P9-DCP-202

$795

# Child Psychology

*A Behavioral Approach to Everyday Problems*

## Roger W. McIntire

UNIVERSITY OF MARYLAND

ILLUSTRATIONS BY GERRIE BLAKE

*BEHAVIORDELIA, INC.*
*Kalamazoo, Michigan*

Copyright © 1970, 1975
Behaviordelia, Inc.
PO Box 1044
Kalamazoo, Michigan   49005

All rights reserved.  No portions
of this book may be reproduced
in any form without permission
from the publisher.

Formerly **For Love of Children.**
Revised Edition.
1st printing — January, 1975

Standard Book Number:
ISBN  0-914-47414-6

Printed and bound by:
R. R. Donnelley and Sons
2223 Martin Luther King Drive
Chicago, Illinois   60616

The author would like to express
gratitude to Ms. Marcie Smith for
her efforts in the preparation of
the figures and manuscript, and to
Dr. Neil Kent, of Western Michigan
University, for his contribution in
developing the objectives that
appear in this text.

The staff involved in the preparation
of this revised edition are:
Elizabeth L. C. Wolf — Senior Editor
David J. Burchell — Technical Editor
Richard W. Malott — Consulting Editor
Dan Hook — Art Direction
Susan Wiltse — Composition
Sharon Sattler — Business Manager

To my wife, Carol,
who not only contributed extensively
to this book but also contributed
its first three subjects.

# Contents

# Roger W. McIntire

*Dr. McIntire brings to the field of child psychology both depth of scholarship and breadth of experience. Since 1962 he has worked in parent-counseling programs, and he has directed research on the behavior problems of children in public schools and teen-agers and adults in institutions.*

*Dr. McIntire, who received his Ph.D. at Louisiana State University in 1962, teaches psychology at the University of Maryland, in addition to participating in various counseling programs supported by private, governmental, and church groups. From his work in these programs and his experiences as a father of three the material and examples in this book have been gathered.*

# Preface

For many years psychologists have searched for solutions to the problems of raising children. Their searches have usually focused on the reasons children might have for doing the things they do. If all these reasons could be discovered, perhaps the discoveries could be used to make changes. But the solutions have been difficult to come by because they seem buried in a maze of complicated answers to the question, "Why do children do the things they do?"

Children do things for a variety of reasons, including past learning, heredity, past treatment, and individual traumatic experiences. All these factors are real and have effects, but knowledge of all of them does not necessarily help parents in search of a practical solution to a specific problem. The explanations that relate to past events may help avoid *future* problems, but the problems that are *here now* can be dealt with only by controlling the here and now.

One rather simple explanation of why children do what they do is that it gets them what they want. It is a simple answer when broadly stated, but when it is applied to figuring out what a child wants in a particular situation it can be complicated.

This book is intended to help you discover the wants of children, and to help you discover how to satisfy those wants through strategies that provide incentives, or rewards, for proper behavior. When parents or teachers take control of such rewards, there is no need for them to feel that they are using some new and potentially cruel power. Satisfying the needs and wants of the child has always been the parents' role. And the child's role has always been to adjust his behavior to obtain these satisfactions from his parents, his teachers, and others. Usually he does this by pleasing these people around him, but he may have to make them angry, embarrassed, or simply tired before they give in and provide him with the things he wants.

So the crucial question confronting parents and teachers is not whether rewards, punishments, encouragements, and discouragements should be used to influence the child's behavior. In day-today living, that influence is inevitable. The question is whether some of the adults around the child will have time and love enough to plan these consequences that will help him learn to grow up properly.

I have taken the view here that childhood and adolescence should be realistic experiences, and I have assumed that such experiences come from the consequences of the child's behavior. Consequences are the most important determinants of the habits of the child. How he acts in a situation depends upon the results he received the last time he was in the same situation. As he experiences similar consequences over and over again, he adjusts his behavior and reacts more consistently.

In this book I have assumed that both you and I want children to grow up and deal with the consequences of the adult world — not tomorrow and not at the expense of missing childhood, but as a result of experience *within* it.

R.W.M.

# Part I

# PARENTHOOD
# BY DESIGN

# 1 / *Strategies for Action*

Your reactions continually influence the behavior and habits of your children. If a child screams in your ear while you're driving, your scolding has an effect. The child may feel ignored at the moment, and he may settle for a scolding to get your attention. If he wants his sister to be quiet, the scolding may accomplish that, even though it is not directed at her. Or scolding him may take attention away from his sister. He may like that. In any of these cases, the reaction he wants is his reason for screaming.

Some of your reactions are insignificant, because they have to do with relatively unimportant actions of your children. But some are important enough to require planning, because they influence crucial habits. Perhaps you have attempted such planning before but have found theories and explanations concerning child psychology too vague to give practical solutions to problems. Such theories frequently give accurate descriptions of particular behaviors but little practical advice about how to deal with specific problems. When you have been told, for example, that your daughter is "introverted" or that your son is "behind for his age," what can you do about it? Some answers might be: "Nothing can be done, because the child was born 'shy' or 'slow,' " or, "He learned to act this way at an early age." To say that he was born shy or slow or that he was "conditioned" at an early age is to say that nothing can be done. To say that nothing can be done is unrealistic, because *something* will be done. The parent *will* react somehow the next time his daughter acts shy or his son ends his homework in failure. Even ignoring the problem is a reaction.

In spite of the way they were born or conditioned, children make continual adjustments to the reactions of their parents. One mother, for example, turned from a backyard talk with a neighbor to deal with her son, who was screaming, "Mommy! Mommy! Mommy!" She yelled back at him, "All right! What is it?" He said, "Hi!" and ran away. She rewarded his nonsense with attention he did not deserve. And she gave him an example of yelling by yelling herself. Yet when she turned back to her neighbor, she said, "Boys will be boys!" She meant that he was yelling because he was born a boy. She may be partly correct, but she is not correct to use that explanation as an excuse for her son's behavior or as an excuse for her failure to do anything to change that behavior.

Explanations and theories, then, may vividly describe what a child is or how he was born or conditioned, but the purpose of this book is to help parents find practical solutions to individual problems.

In the past twenty years, psychology has concentrated on changes in individual behaviors. One group of psychologists, known as behaviorists, believe that because such "inside events" as mental processes and emotions cannot be seen, it is difficult to reach agreement about which ones are happening and when. Consequently, behaviorists attempt to explain activities of the child by dealing with the outside events—what the child does and what the world does to the child. When behaviors are bad, they are examined not as symptoms of deeper problems but as the result of other outside events: the experiences of the child.

## What's Happening?

If you attempt to get at real problems without concentrating on the child's behavior and experiences, you make a common mistake, for in mere speculation about the child there is no plan of action. You might describe a certain teen-ager as moody, disrespectful, rebellious, or cynical. You might speculate that this trait is part of growing up and say, "That's the way it is with kids nowadays." But the teen-ager may act disrespectfully because in his past experience the only time he was taken seriously was when he spoke in this way. When he is happy and cheerful, adults may pat him on the head and tell him he's a "nice boy" but otherwise ignore him. To become cynical about "kids nowadays" is to miss the crucial point that college presidents (and parents) pay more attention to rioting students than they do to nonrioting students.

We can be distracted and delayed from working out better reactions to the teen-ager's occasional moments of cheerfulness by dwelling on his inner "rebellious feelings." This description merely sidetracks us from doing something to change the behavior. To change the teen-ager's moodiness we must find out what events created it. What reactions does he get for disrespect? What could be changed to stop it? Or replace it? These questions will lead to some practical plans for bringing about a change.

Concentrating on behaviors allows us to discover how to use our reactions to change behavior. The more recognizable the activity is, the more consistent the reactions to it can be and therefore the more consistent the child's experience and learning. For example, parents can easily agree on when their child is attempting to walk and thus when to help him with the task. A behavioral description here is easy ("Whenever he stands up and moves his feet around"), and parents usually agree on how and when to encourage him.

Parents often disagree, however, about whether a child is angry because he wants attention or because he is tired. Often, even one parent cannot decide how to react. How can he know how to react to "angry" when he is not sure what the behavior means? If the father wants the homework finished, he may decide that the child is merely trying to get attention. If the mother wants to get the child off to bed so that she can relax, she may decide that he is tired and not just trying to get attention. Because the parents cannot agree on what "acting angry" means, they see what they want to see and find themselves disagreeing. So there is confusion even about such simple characteristics as fatigue and anger. For this reason, behaviorists feel that such abstract terms as "shy," "mean," "loving," and "impatient" must be defined further before parents can agree on what their child is doing. Then, with concrete definitions, parents can decide what to do about the problem.

An insistence on *describing* outside behavior is important, then, because it tends to make parents think in useful and concrete ways. It allows them to agree about what their children do. Considering how to encourage a child who is "shy," for example, is a complex problem. Such a popular or abstract description of a person does not explain the little events that make up the average day. It is too large and covers too many activities and habits. Parents must know what behaviors to look for so that they can pinpoint what worries them. If they restate the problem of shyness as "He doesn't talk very much" or "He hides when company comes," then the chances of knowing when they should consistently apply some encouragement are increased.

Another advantage of describing behaviors is that the description reveals what must be practiced for there to be improvement. Any person's behavior is consistent with his experiences—his successes and failures in the past. We learn from practice, from having tried things in the past and having benefited from those trials. Thus, a behavioristic description is not just a way of agreeing about the child; it is also a fundamental law of learning: *One learns what one does.* The things we practice are the things that we learn best. Anyone who has ever tried to learn to play golf or bridge or to raise children knows that just talking about how to do it is not enough. There are rules to be read before progress can be made, but the progress itself—the result—will have to come from experience and practice. So it is with children. Helping a child to listen and to pay attention is not enough. He will have to try your instructions, test your rules, and then, *if the consequences are consistently as you say they will be*, he will change.

## Practice Makes Almost Perfect

Learning has to do with practice. It is a result of experience. It is a change in behavior *due to practice*. For example, overt practice before tests—such as reading aloud, talking with others about the work, or rewriting notes from a lecture or text, and so on—is the best way for students to learn and to prepare for exams. Those who are skeptical of this strategy should try the following experiment: Pick out a popular magazine that you enjoy in which there are at least two stories or articles you have not yet read. Read the first story to yourself in your usual way. Find someone who is free at the moment and tell him the story, including the details— who was in it, what they were doing, what their names were, and so on. Now go back to the magazine and read a second story, but this time stand up, hold the magazine in front of you, and read *aloud*—to the wall if necessary. Now find someone and repeat this story by giving all the facts about characters, activities, and places. Usually by the end of the second trial, people observe how much more they can remember of the second story when they are retelling it. As one student put it, "Well, of course I remember it. I remember having *said* it." For the purpose of learning or changing habits, there is no substitute for actively practicing behaviors.

We all seem to understand the necessity for practice when teaching something to a very young child or when teaching someone to play a musical instrument. But when we are not teaching such things as tying a shoelace, playing the piano, and hitting a baseball, we often forget that practice is the essential ingredient of change. This principle applies just as well to bed making, dish washing, talking, manners, and other social skills. If you do these jobs for a child, then he does not practice. A child can be overprotected by giving him too much help ("I'll cut the meat," "I'll pour the milk," "I'll read—you listen," "I'll call and see if your friend can come over—you wait"). This protection keeps the child from actually becoming involved and doing things himself. You can see that if you allow it to happen, the child can gain a lot of practice every day.

Some practice happens by accident; some requires your planning. For example, learning how to use a spoon at dinner comes from using it in the sandbox as well as at the dinner table. Learning to use words to describe activities and experiences may require planned practice as well as accidental practice. Learning to talk well comes as much from engaging in conversations as from listening to the reading of stories or comics. But in the last case, practice may or may not be allowed by the parent. The child can be asked to *tell* the story of the Sunday comic to the parent after the parent has read it to him. Listening is not practice for the child. If the comics are simple ("Henry" or "Mr. Mum," for example), the child can tell the story himself. He can retell the more complicated ones after they have been read. In this way the practice lets *the child* learn to enjoy comics, and he learns more about talking and explaining things to other people.

When parents do not allow practice, painful experiences are ahead for their child. Consider, for example, a girl whose parents have allowed her very little practice and have made all her decisions for her—when to go to bed, what to wear, where to wear it, when to eat, and so on. As this girl leaves for college, her first long stay away from home by herself, she probably receives more instructions than ever before ("Make sure you brush your teeth," "Keep your hair combed," "Get plenty of sleep"). She has been allowed to make few discriminations for herself and has only been verbally instructed; she has not had the benefit of making many mistakes in practice. She has had little contact with the consequences that would ordinarily occur for her behaviors in the outside world because she has never been allowed the advantage of making mistakes and reaping the consequences. So when she goes away to school, she becomes homesick because she does not know what to wear, how to iron her clothes, when to study, when to take a break, or when to go to bed. She may go to a student counselor with the complaint that no one seems to care about her in the big university. Certainly there may be truth in her complaint against the modern university, but a great deal of the care she misses should have been gradually withdrawn years ago to make room for practice. Now there is no one close enough to her who loves her enough to spend time and energy directing her every move.

## Small Steps and Big Rewards

Perhaps you have found that in learning to play a musical instrument even practice was not enough. But do you remember that in perfecting handwriting, practice *was* eventually enough to produce successful learning? What differences are there between playing the piano and improving handwriting? In learning to improve handwriting there are rewards not only for the result of hours of practice but even for the first little successes. The letters immediately look better when practiced. But to improve the sound of a scale or a song, hours or weeks of practice are needed. Rewards are not immediate. If rewards come for the first little successes, then a child will want to work ahead on other small steps. But when rewards come only after big successes, a child becomes discouraged along the way and wants to stop. He may say, "I'll never be really good." It is not the pot at the end of the rainbow that keeps the behavior going—it's the next pat on the back or penny in the bank.

In the cases of handwriting and piano playing, the parents usually have not planned any reward. But usually handwriting is successfully learned, whereas piano playing may not be. Why is this true? The parents usually reward the first successes in writing as worthwhile accomplishments in themselves. And the parents are right. The first successful writing is useful and worthwhile. But the first little ditties learned in piano playing are not, *in themselves*, very useful or worthwhile; the parents and the child know this, and the result is that little reward occurs. Writing one's own name, or a friend's name, or a secret message is an important and rewarding accomplishment, and it is continually practiced. The response to a successful playing of the scale, however, may be a half-hearted compliment or complete indifference. To overcome the lack of rewards for beginning steps of behavior, practice should be rewarded by something obvious and valuable. Perhaps learning a favorite or popular song with one finger should be an early part of the lessons. That way, success with these lessons will attract attention and encouragement.

## EXPERIMENT 1

### Consequences at Home

Jerry[1] hated wearing the head band that pressed against the braces on his teeth. It was necessary if his teeth were ever to be straightened, but he would only wear the device 25% of the time. Four dentists who were paid $3300 over eight years had failed to correct his problem.

Jerry's mother enrolled in a behavior modification class for parents and selected this problem as her project. First she tried praising Jerry when he wore the device (social reward). Then she tried ignoring rather than nagging him when he wasn't wearing it. Next she told Jerry he would get 25 cents every time she checked and found the device in place. She kept a record, and Jerry was paid monthly. This was later changed to a daily payoff.

Jerry's performance didn't show any change during social reward. However, the device was in place 60% of the time for monthly payoffs and 97% for daily payoffs. Over a period of 70 days, she decreased the number of times she checked the device, but performance remained almost perfect.

The most common error when beginning to teach something new to a child is to demand too much for too small a reward. The first little steps need big rewards. "But this is bribery," you say. "Shouldn't a child do most of these things without reward, just for the joy of learning? Some children are good and do what is expected without any reward, don't they?" To answer this question you must first realize that those good little children are rewarded—socially—a great deal. Some children start early and well, with plenty of social encouragement. They now perform so well that they receive a great deal of praise, which has a snowballing effect. If a child starts off well, he is well rewarded; if he is well rewarded, he keeps going; if he keeps going, he is further rewarded, and so on.

Snowballing can work the other way too. Some children have not been rewarded for being good or learning. They do not expect rewards because they have not received them in the past. If a child starts slowly or poorly on something, he misses a lot of encouragement and gets badgering instead. The lack of rewards

---

Ten-year-old Antoinette flatly refused to do her household chores. Nagging and punishment didn't help. Then Antoinette's mother placed a chart in her daughter's bedroom which showed the number of "merit" points that could be earned. The chart went into exact detail as to what must be done in each case. If her bed was made Mom put up five points. If her clothes were hung up — five points. If her dresser was neat — five points. If her floor was swept — five points. If she dusted the living room -- ten points. If she washed dishes — twenty points. Antoinette improved only slightly. She made 10 to 20 merit points each day. However, when points were exchanged for pennies her average jumped to 36.7! Then her mother arranged to exchange points for a Campfire uniform and accessories (400 points for a blouse, etc.), and her average went up to 42.2 points per day.

Claire was a five-year-old who took from one to seven hours to dress herself. When she lost her T.V. privileges if she wasn't dressed within 30 minutes, her average dressing time dropped to 23 minutes!

slows him down even more as he gets older. Performance that would have been rewarded is not encouraged, because "He should have been doing that years ago, anyway."

In both cases the rewards for good behavior and the lack of rewards are important. So we cannot say that some children need reward and some do not. <u>All of them need reward.</u>

Does this mean that all successful parents are bribers—black-mailers? No. First, these words are unfair because they imply a situation in which a person is trying to corrupt another person so that he will do something that is wrong and usually illegal.

Second, we are all interested in some return for our effort. None of us does anything for nothing. The reward may be as subtle as another person saying we are doing good for others, but it is there from time to time to keep us going. On one occasion a father rejected a plan for correcting his son's behavior by saying, "He should be grown-up enough to want to do the right thing without some payoff." When the counselor thanked the father for taking time off from work to come and talk with him, the father answered, "Oh, that's all right. We're on strike for a raise this week, anyway." He felt differently when his "payoff" was involved. Because of his experience and knowledge he felt he deserved a tangible reward—more money. His son, without much experience, was to take his responsibilities for the love of it. This father feels so superior to his son that he not only views their capabilities as different but also views their needs as different. In a word: he is prejudiced.

We all carry prejudice against the young with us. They are less capable and, if cared for by parents, they are in less need. Therefore, the payoff for them can be less because of less need and, responsibility and opportunity to perform can be less because they are less capable. As with most prejudice, the view is carried to extreme. Because a child needs *less* money from day to day he may be allowed to earn *no* money. Because he is *less* capable of cooking he is allowed to do *no* cooking. Once this extreme view is taken no learning can occur because there is no incentive and no practice. Isn't there an easy starting place even for the child who has fallen far behind? And couldn't some encouragement be arranged for his smallest successes?

In order for a boy who is behind his grade level at school to catch up there will have to be sufficient rewards for him, just as there are for everyone else. Practice will have to be accompanied by rewards. As we are using the word here, "practice" does not mean merely the repeating of behavior; it also refers to the consequences for the behaviors. Parents must provide the consequences and allow the child to practice the behavior in his own way. This procedure can be tiresome, but it is important. It is frustrating to the parent to let the child do the task and foul it up. It is so much easier to make a seven-year-old's bed than to watch him make a mess of it; it is so much easier to tell a ten-year-old girl what to wear than to send her back to her room four times to replace inappropriate clothing.

The situation may be particularly difficult when it is also necessary to provide enthusiastic encouragement and reward for poor approximations of the ideal behavior, but the need to give constant encouragement and reward is absolutely imperative in this kind of practice. It would be nice if, after a little practice, a child would continue to perform on his own, but he will not. You will have to continue to be a rewarding parent. Even the boy who continually builds model airplanes, despite his apparently natural motivation to do it for hours on end, still needs admiration for his work in order to continue good work. For more difficult behaviors—homework, manners, sociability—opportunities for practice *and* rewards must be provided. This is the big job for parents. It requires concern, study, and time, and it is often discouraging. It requires love.

## *OBJECTIVES*   *chapter one*

1. How do behaviorists differ from child psychologists who consider bad behaviors symptoms of deeper problems?

2. What are two advantages gained when parents focus on the outside behavior of their children?

3. Practice is an essential ingredient of change. Define practice.

4. Explain the importance of giving "the first little steps" big rewards.

5. What is the difference between a reward and a bribe?

6. Why is it necessary for parents to reward a child's behavior even if the behavior is not perfect?

# 2 / Planning Ahead

In *The Gesell Institute's Child Behavior*, you are advised to "try to provide, so far as you can, the kind of situation in which each kind of child can feel comfortable and can do well. But don't try to change him and make him over." The advice is good except that the words "kind of situation" and "doing well" are not definite enough to tell you what to do. The following chapters describe the kinds of situations you can provide. As a matter of fact, you are providing some kind of situation for your child now, and it does "change him and make him over." Now you must plan that situation so that it influences him in the way you think best.

The way in which a child gains independence may vary from family to family. We all would probably agree that ideally child rearing should be a process of gradually expanding responsibility, practice, activity, and independence. Unfortunately, however, for most children there is a long period of "limitations" followed by an abrupt change in the number of activities for which he is held responsible. For example, the American teenager experiences being thrown out of the nest at about age seventeen, when he goes off for a life of his own—to college or work.

While living at home most teen-agers experience very little practice with consequences given by people outside the family. Once away from home, teen-agers learn quickly from the severe application of consequences by the culture. Most of those teenagers grow up late, painfully, and abruptly—but they grow up. As the newspapers tell us, however, there are many young adults who do not do very well during their sudden plunge into independence. Many do not have the social behaviors so valued by the adult world. They question and reject the rationale for behaviors that the adult world values and expects. Because they face an adjustment to everything at once, they find it too much to cope with; it is easier for them to reject society.

Probably one of the common reasons for such total rejection is that their parents never showed them the meaning and value of many behaviors through practice. The parents did not allow their children the freedom to make some of their own decisions and reap the consequences for those decisions. If making decisions and reaping consequences are allowed regularly, teen-agers experience the success and failure of their decisions. After successes the parents rejoice with the teen-agers; after failures parents give support by pointing out and helping them explore the use of alternate behaviors. A long period of trial and error is possible for children whose parents are willing to allow it. When the young adult leaves home without this practice, there is no time for discussion, exploration, or selection (or for rejection). While rushing into adulthood, there is no time to pick and choose.

## Rules Within Reason

Very young children do not usually show extreme resistance to the values of society, because they find natural gratification in the things they are rewarded for by their parents. It is naturally gratifying to be successful in dressing oneself, in tying one's shoelaces, or in overpowering and successfully using a spoon. In these cases the genuine usefulness of the activity is a great advantage to the parent. But how quickly the obvious worth of tasks can become blurred and debatable. After mastering the spoon, the next lesson is table manners. After successful dressing is learned, the next lesson is proper selection of clothes. The parent must examine the reasoning behind rules and customs about behavior, or he will be edged into the uncomfortable position of defending an arbitrary selection of behaviors to be learned. His own value system is threatened, in a very small way, but it is an ominous preview of the confrontations to come in the next fifteen to twenty years.

At one time or another all parents fail to work out in their own minds the justification for some of their procedures. When questioned, they find themselves rationalizing in a desperate attempt to protect their own authority and to quell childish rebellion. A justification can be more than a wall against invasion. Many advantages are gained by working out the reason for concern about certain behaviors. We are creatures of habit. We may continue to react to a common circumstance in an inconvenient and unpleasant way for reasons that have not been reviewed for years. Consider, for example, poor posture in the teen-ager. This behavior prompts a great deal of nagging, pleading, and threatening. The parent makes himself unpleasant in these reactions not only to the child but to himself. A great deal of the family time is clouded with verbal jabs. A frank discussion about why posture is a behavior of concern might result in one of the conclusions that follow. Some of these conclusions might apply to many of the behaviors that concern you.

1. The behavior is too trivial to bother with. Let's ignore it and thereby eliminate a lot of unpleasant gibing and make more time for other kinds of talk.
2. The justification is off in the future. When he starts "noticing" girls, he'll straighten up and care about his appearance. Knowing that, let's give up and wait for the girls to do it.

3. The behavior really is worth changing. Let's think up a consequence that will work and stop all this nagging. From now on,
anyone in the family caught slouching must immediately put a
penny in the jar on the kitchen table. Anyone completing a
day without having to put in a penny may take 10 cents from
the jar (Mom or Dad pays off if the jar is empty—a small price
to pay).

4. The behavior really is worth changing, and it hasn't changed
because the child knows that he is getting through to us. There
is already a reward working; it is the very nagging and pleading that we thought would reduce the behavior. (The answer
here is the same as in conclusion 1, above.)

5. The behavior is worth changing because *we* would find it
more pleasant that way. It is not for the child's sake, but for
ours. The penny jar will be used as much for our sake as for
his.

The last position can be valid, as shown in the following
situation: "Mom and Dad, why can't I stay out late on all three
nights of the weekend—Friday, Saturday, and Sunday?" Is it
because one of those nights must be used for homework? If this is
true and if he shows you there is no homework, may he stay out
all three nights? Is it to force him to get his rest? Then why does
Dad want him up so early on Saturday morning? Sometimes the
genuine justification underlying this kind of rule is that the
parents want one evening when they may have peace of mind and
do not have to worry about where their son is. If this reason were
stated frankly—"I want you here one night so I don't have to
worry about it"—most of the arguments above would be avoided.
Selfishness can be justified under these circumstances, but dishon-
esty cannot. Parents must continually police themselves about
honesty and should begin before their children become teen-
agers. If the five-year-old cannot go running and screaming
through the house, don't tell him that it is because nice boys don't
do things like that if the real reason is that it annoys Dad.

As you get down to these real reasons for your requests, begin a list of the important behaviors that you want your child to have. Also make a list of his behaviors that you're unhappy with. Keep the list in order, the behaviors of greatest concern at the top, the more trivial at the bottom. When you decide that a behavior is trivial make a special effort to remove all special consequences for it. Stop all nagging and reprimanding. React as you would to another adult when this trivial behavior occurs. Make this decision work for you by clearing the air and removing the ugly nagging, and end reprimanding aimed at behaviors which you've already tagged as unimportant. Even before you begin a program of rewards for good behaviors, eliminate the special consequences for trivial behaviors and you will make the family more positive, and your home a more free and pleasant place to live.

## EXPERIMENT 2

### Using Consequences To Deal with Bad Behavior

Rorey[2] was a screaming, fighting, disobedient, bossy, only child. He settled down partially at pre-school (he was four-and-a-half), but was a terror at home. The family physician thought Rorey had a severe emotional problem. His problem behaviors were listed as: physical aggression (hitting, pushing, kicking, throwing objects, biting, and scratching); yelling; bossiness (telling other children what to do); and disobedience.

Rorey's mother followed each occurrence of bad behavior with a visit to the time out (TO) room.

Each time Rorey was taken to TO, social interaction was held to a minimum. An example of a comment would be, "You cannot stay here if you fight." The room had neither toys nor anything else of interest. Rorey was kept there with the door latched for only two minutes on each visit. This was to be a consequence — a repeatable consequence — which was to help Rorey learn through practice. A longer time out would have been abusive and would have allowed too little time for practice. Rorey improved. He was disobedient 10% instead of 70% of the time. He was aggressive 1% rather than 10% of the time. He was loud or bossy 8% rather than 25% of the time.

## The Parent as Patsy

To select a consequence and say, "If you are not nice today, you will not go to the circus on Saturday," is to ignore the principle of practiced experience. Going to the circus is a reward but, like successful piano playing, it is too far off. Not only is it too far off, it cannot be repeated. At least if a child makes some progress in piano playing, he might begin to pick up repeated rewards. But this one shot cannot be used with consistency, because it occurs only once. Either you do or do not take the child to the circus. It is as if you were trying to hold off a thousand Indians with a rifle that has only one bullet in it; the only hope under these circumstances would be to use a lot of verbal threats without ever following through. It's the same way with children: Once you follow through, you've had it. If you refuse the trip to the circus, you are an ogre; if you do not follow through, you are a patsy. Either way, you lose. And the day after the circus you have nothing to use and you lose again. Allow yourself and your family to enjoy individual treats without trying to use them to limit bad behavior. It is better to choose and contrive something that can be applied *frequently*, something that is not so severe that it can only be a threat.

For example, don't continually threaten to throw away all the toys that you have to pick up (a threat so severe that it is unmanageable). Designate a "weekly toy closet" in which all toys that are picked up by the parents will be placed. The closet will be unlocked at a certain time of the week, so that all the toys of the week can be reclaimed by their owners. If that event takes place on Monday night, any toy picked up by the parents on Tuesday or thereafter is placed in the toy closet and of course is not available until the closet is unlocked again next Monday night. With this procedure you will have a repeatable consequence that can become a consistent and more reasonable experience to the child and therefore bring about a consistent change. A very repeatable consequence makes it much easier to refrain from nagging. The repetition and reminding is done not by a nagging parent but by the consequence itself. Nagging can stop, and use of a regular consequence can begin—a consequence that is not just a one shot or so severe as to be unreasonable.

Now you are off to a good start. You are thinking in terms of repeated consequences and their effect upon a specific and observable behavior. You have some idea of what questions must be asked, and you know that the consequences that are going to be used must be reasonable, honest, and repeatable.

There is little doubt that you have already formed some habits about consequences in your daily activities with your children. These habits are not planned consequences, but they represent your tendency to react to your children in a certain way.

How easily and how frequently *do* you react to your children? Everyone has seen parents who are riding their children all the time: "Blow your nose," "Tuck in your shirt," "Don't touch," and so on. On the other hand, we have also seen parents who *never* react; they let their children run wild. Both extremes raise many questions. For example, one way of viewing the pleasantness and the friendliness of a parent or any other person is to consider his tendency to support, encourage, agree with, or in other ways give rewards frequently. These jovial and approachable people seem to have a rule that says, "When in doubt, reward. Hardly ever punish." To the extent that you correct, contradict, reprimand, and punish, you lose this friendly air. The reason a teen-ager would rather go out with friends than stay home with his family is usually this difference in the likelihood that his behavior will be accepted (rewarded). This anticipation may explain why a fifteen-year-old boy will leave a warm and comfortable home to stand on a cold street corner with buddies for an evening.

On the other hand, a very low frequency of consequences or a complete lack of requirements will provide no information about rights and wrongs and there will be no limits. All children and adults continually explore limits; if there are none, things may get out of hand.

No doubt the most effective reward used in the home is the verbal praise and encouragement given by the parents. When this praise is consistently used in an obvious manner for a particular behavior, results are gratifying. It cannot be emphasized enough how much your attention influences the behavior of your children. Attention, praise, and general encouragement are handy rewards. They are given often. Your child attracts your attention easily. Therefore, this attention is the most powerful influence on your child's behavior. Because attention is so influential, the question arises of what behaviors should *not* attract it. Selecting the behaviors to be rewarded or ignored is the main business of being a parent.

Although most of the time we are reacting without any plan, there will have to be some rules about rewards and some about punishment. To decide, for example, to correct, reprimand, or punish *every* wrong behavior is to be an unpleasant person. If you are set to correct nearly every mistake your child makes when he talks to you, you probably also complain that he does not talk to you much. It is more desirable to reward (by nodding approval or smiling, for example) the little mistakes than to punish at a high frequency and in an unplanned, unpurposeful way. That way there will still be a behavior to work with later. You will also have a child who is still informative, friendly, and willing to spend some time with you.

The choice between rewards and punishments will be discussed in detail in Chapter 5, but in most cases the odds favor reward. Furthermore, because you should maintain a positive, friendly relationship with your children, the when-in-doubt-reward rule is probably a good basic one. Punishment shows that out of all the responses the child could have made, his was the wrong one—try again. Punishment, then, is inefficient because it gives little information about what correct behavior is. Reward is much more efficient, because it says that out of all the responses he could have made, his was the desired one. It is more difficult to use reward, however, because you must take the time to decide what you want to reward, whereas you probably already know what you want to punish.

## Do as I Do . . .

If you find it difficult to know what good behaviors *you* want from your children, then you can see how difficult it is going to be for them to find out how they should behave. What will they try first? Most of the time they will try out what you do. If it works for you, perhaps it will work for them. Just as you always provide consequences for your children, so are you always a potential example to them. There may be some question whether they will be rewarded for imitating your example, but they probably will be. You have found that your behavior is the best adjustment for you, so they probably will too; you will show your agreement with them, and that will be a reward. As one mother once said, "I can't understand why my children fuss at each other all the time. I'm always fussing at them about it!"

## EXPERIMENT 3

### Consequences at Camp and Zoo

Tooth-brushing[3] was a problem at Camp Kidsareaway. Only 10% of the ten-to-twelve-year-old boys there brushed. However, when the counselors promised an afternoon swim if brushing occurred after the noon meal, 100% of the boys brushed on most occasions, but only after the noon meal. When the counselors dropped the brushing requirement for swimming, brushing fell back toward zero.

Littering[4] was a problem at the Woodland Park Zoo. The director had a sign placed over a trash can which read, "At times, persons depositing litter in this container will be rewarded.", and Pepsi coupons were given out as the reward. Litter deposits increased sixfold.

In another case, a father and mother sought help in dealing with their teen-ager, whose main difficulty was his disrespect for others, particularly his mother. "Disrespect" was defined as making sarcastic remarks, ignoring direct questions, and insulting people. The father said he thought the mother contributed to this behavior by being "wishy-washy" and not "standing up to him, even if she was a woman." He thought she probably got this attitude from spending time in "big conferences" with some of the "silly neighbors." It was easy to see the example the father had set for the son to imitate. And because he imitated his father, the son expected praise and admiration for his behavior.

PARENTAL DISPOSITION  /  Thus, the child's disposition is usually a copy of parental attitude. This copying is almost always rewarded by the parents because, after all, they have found their way best. The disposition to punish and correct others can be learned just as easily as the disposition to reward them. The general disposition of the family thus is a critical factor affecting consequences, and if it is negative, the parents should hold a strategy session to determine the example to be set and the timing of rewards.

## EXPERIMENT 4

### Modeling

Thirteen socially withdrawn children[5] who interacted least with their fellow nursery-school classmates were observed during the school day. They were rated along with the rest of the class each time they looked at or interacted with another child.

The children were then shown a film of 11 scenes of children enjoying and being rewarded for pleasant interaction with other children. The narrator emphasized the good behaviors. The scenes progressed from small quiet interactions to large groups playing energetically.

The results showed that the socially withdrawn children copied those in the film. Number of interactions with other children increased as much as 500% over that behavior before the film.

To police your "disposition" through a planned strategy is a difficult task. There are no planned consequences for *you* built into it, and you change by practice with consequences just as children do. So whether or not anything can be done about the dispositions in your home is reflected in the answer to the question "Can this mother and father *plan* to control a little of each other's behavior through social consequences?" If this change is possible—if one parent can truthfully say to the other, "Don't let me pick on the kids; stop me and point out my good reactions to them"—then there is hope for change in disposition and family atmosphere.

The disposition of the family can also be influenced by making plans about the small social behaviors of the children. Many parents have gained their bad dispositions from not planning the limits of their demands upon their children. In what situations, for example, will the child be on his own? A child makes so many mistakes; there are so many things we want him to do right, and so many things he can do wrong. So, without planning, the parent feels he has to be after the child every minute just to avoid disaster. "She just can't leave him alone," says the father. This difficulty arises because the mother attempts to correct and instruct her child about many behaviors that she has never really discussed or planned to correct. Her habit of correcting others usually develops into the habit of telling others what to do in advance so that they won't make so many mistakes.

This situation was most evident one day while a mother and her son were waiting in a counselor's office while he finished other work. The things that happened indicated what the problem was even before it was discussed. The boy came in first and sat on a convenient chair; the mother chose to sit at the opposite side of the waiting area. "Sit over here," she said. (Why was it necessary for him to sit next to her?) "Don't swing your foot." The boy picked up a book from the table. "Be careful with that," she said. The boy turned a page noisily. "Shh," she said. The situation seemed similar to a dog show in which the man exhibiting the German shepherd wants to show the judge how completely he dominates and controls every move of the dog. The mother was even less justified in displaying such control than the dog trainer because she didn't even plan to do it. As it turned out, one of her complaints was that her son was bossy with other children.

An interesting aspect of such a disposition is that generally a parent uses it only with her child. She does not ordinarily act this way with other people. Rather, she has come to expect something different of her own child and nags about the slightest deviations from her expectation. But the expectation itself has not been worked out, nor has it been planned for. What at first appears to be a high standard or high expectation is actually *no specific* standard or expectation at all. The parent punishes nearly everything and leaves no opportunity for good behavior.

This type of disposition is almost always the result of a lack of planning and attention to parental reactions. The critical part of the planning that is left out is the designation of the important behaviors as opposed to the trivial behaviors. Had the mother in the counselor's office ever thought about whether her son should always sit next to her? She said that she had not. Why had she instructed him to do so? After some guessing she said she was afraid he would "do something wrong over there." She had no specific expectation of his doing something wrong; she just did not trust her son. Some boys might have deserved such mistrust, but for this boy it was just habit with a little reprimand built in. A psychological leash had been placed on the boy, and it was jerked very often.

To break the habit of using a psychological leash a good rule to include in your strategy is "Don't correct or instruct your child until you *know* he will make a mistake." This is a rule that all adults expect you to apply to them, and your child deserves as much of your faith as any adult deserves. Train yourself to hesitate before giving a reprimanding consequence or correction. Is your child really doing or about to do something wrong? Is the reprimand likely to function as a reward for bad behavior? Is this the attitude you want your child to learn from you?

In addition to creating a general atmosphere, disposition affects planning about particular problems. In the day-to-day activities of the family, for example, certain questions continually crop up. The child considers them very important and, although he knows the answers, he continually harps on them. "But Mommy, why *can't* I walk to the movies alone?" "I already told you why." "I know, but can't I? Pleeease!" "No." The next day it starts all over again. "Mommy, Mary wants me to walk to the movies with her. Can I go?" What events maintain this behavior? It is a topic that always brings disagreement and punishment, but it is always brought up.

The first and most likely reason for this running battle is that the mother and father have never held a brief planning session about the problem. Without this strategy session the reasons given to the child change from time to time; the parents disagree from time to time; and both lose confidence in these decisions from time to time. The inconsistency encourages the child to keep trying so that one day he might hit the right combination of times and get to go. He probably will.

The planning session would nail down the reasons, pinpoint the agreement between the parents and give them confidence. It would help by stating in detail the honest reasons for the decision. "Your mother and I have decided you can't walk to the movies alone. We think bigger people will bother you and make trouble for you along the way and while you're there. When you are ten, you may do it. Right, Martha?" Mother says, "Yes." Now, will he stop nagging? Probably not, but the amount of nagging will decrease, and the child will be happier because the situation is now clear, honest, and fair. To be given the structure, to know what's what, is much more comfortable than to be punished and argued with continually. The child's behavior will change because the statement of the rule is concrete and detailed.

After the air has been cleared a little, make a special effort to reward the good behaviors and conversations you've planned to look for. Don't let this vacuum be filled by some other attention-getting behavior.

Disposition, then, is also a matter of being alert to punish or alert to reward. Looking for bad behaviors and punishing them is, in itself, an aversive activity that forces the parents to be unpleasant. Also, punishment tends to reduce the overall amount of behavior of the child and, therefore, disallow practice. In this way, two general characteristics of love, friendship, and a generally pleasant disposition are violated; the tendency is to punish rather than to give the child the benefit of the doubt, and even when the parent is available, the child's behavior is kept in check by the constant threat of punishment. In the long run, it is usually the good behavior that is reduced by punishment.

It should be emphasized that we are discussing not only physical punishment but also the frequency of those reprimands —those scoldings and sarcastic comments—that are supposedly designed to suppress behavior. We would even include many left-handed compliments, which look like rewards but are really reprimands: "That certainly is a big improvement over last year" or "That's very good, considering . . ."

GUFF / Let us examine the disposition of the child in more detail. You may have already gotten some idea about where your child has come upon some of the examples for his disposition, but you are now in a much better position to deal with this difficulty, because you can determine the behaviors that make it up. The most obvious characteristic of "bad-disposition behavior" is that its consequence is a general reduction in the behavior of its target. The parent can silence the child or keep him from acting up by assuming a threatening pose that implies that if the child does anything, he is likely to be punished. The child uses the same idea, but he is a less powerful figure and must use it in a more subtle way.

"Guff control" is the term we shall use to describe the circumstance in which the parents decide that they would rather do something themselves than "take all that guff." The child uses the guff to put his mother off and to get out of some undesirable request for work. But his behavior is also a result of the fact that the request is *just* work, that is, he is using guff to avoid performing the behavior because the behavior itself doesn't pay off.

By this time you may be getting a little tired of the idea that everything must pay off, but remember that what is meant by "pay off" in many cases is an honest expression after a job is done that it was good and helpful to have it done.

Be careful how you give this expression of appreciation. To say, "Well, that wasn't so bad, was it?" is to misunderstand the use of consequences. You are using success as another opportunity to reprimand the child for delaying. Think of how you would show your appreciation to another adult if he did this task for you. Use that payoff instead of some condescending comment reserved for a child who you think should want to do the task anyway.

So both parent and child usually engage in some bad-disposition behavior; one tries to bring about an activity by coercion and the other avoids that activity because it is straight coercion without any significant reward. When the child is using guff, he often exposes the situation quite well by saying, "Oh, why should I do that?" The statement is pure guff intended to stop some request of the parent, but, incidentally, it asks a very good question. Why should the child do that? The problem in child rearing is that it is much easier to attempt to coerce some behavior through your authority than to plan and provide reasonable, positive consequences. Providing reasonable, positive consequences requires that rules be made and used that will necessitate some planning or—at the very least—a new point of view that allows you to give more social approval with greater ease.

## The Logic of Consequences

Consequences influence future behaviors, and this rule applies to unwanted behaviors as well as desirable behaviors. When a mother first asks why her children fight and argue at home, she expects an answer in terms of their emotional constitution and such determining factors as early experiences and sibling rivalry. If the answer suggests a procedure that would result in a change, however, the "Why?" must be taken to mean "What happens next?" The event that immediately follows the behavior is the consequence that must be observed.

Some close observations will have to be made, and the easiest way to make them is to draw up a small chart on which they can be tallied. Reserve an easily accessible place, perhaps on a kitchen bulletin board, for the chart and nearby attach a pencil on a string. Keeping a precise record of an undesirable behavior and its immediate consequences is well worth the effort, for much more than just a suggestion of consequences will come from it. You will be able to see the time of day when the behavior occurs, with whom it occurs, and its consequences.

In the toilet-training situation, for example, posting a chart over the diaper pail allows parents to record the times of day when diapers are changed so that training can begin as soon as the regular time intervals are determined. When these are known, the child can be put on the toilet at the most opportune times. Successes are noted on the chart so that the child can see, and the parents themselves are encouraged by, concrete evidence of progress. Under these conditions, the desired consequences are much more likely to occur, and the parents do not give up easily, because they see progress, which is their reward.

Such charts thus provide more than information; they provide incentives. When used properly, they remind the child of his past successes as well as reminding the parents to upgrade their expectations of the child's performance and the planned rewards for those higher performances. Charts minimize the probabilities that misunderstandings will occur about when behaviors were performed and when rewards were given. So don't let the complicated process of raising a child depend on the memories and consistencies of two of the people so deeply and emotionally involved in the process itself. Keep records and charts.

The necessity to record detailed sequences means that you will have to single out individual problems; you cannot record everything about your family and yourself at one time. It is impossible to plan rewards and punishments and to carry out the plans for many problems at once. You must select one problem and let the rest of the problems go for the time being. You might, for example, record a mark each time the children fight. You might also record one each time you, the parents, give attention to the uproar. After you give close attention to the problem for a week, the consequences supporting the children's behaviors usually become apparent. Possibly fighting is a "fill-up-time behavior" that occurs when the children have nothing better to do. You might discover this relationship when you observe that your reaction to fighting is to suggest things that will keep them out of trouble. Or fighting may be followed by a parental reprimand and interference, and the children may be fighting for that attention.

It may seem ridiculous at first to think that children would fight to be punished by their parents. But one of the cardinal rules in thinking about consequences is that consequences must be judged by how they affect behavior, not by what parents think their effect should be.

The common tantrum of the two- to five-year-old is an excellent example of the last point. Usually any attention given to the tantrum is a reward for it. You see hints that this is the case when you realize that the probability of a tantrum is greatest when a child is being ignored because company is present or when you are on the telephone or when some competitive situation has developed in which another child has become the focus of attention. Be suspicious of all verbal reprimands, corrections, and even physical punishments. There is always a possibility that they are rewards rather than the punishments they are intended to be. A parent expressed his understanding of his child's goal in throwing a tantrum by saying, "He knows he's getting through to me. He just wants to get my goat. He's just showing off."

## EXPERIMENT 5

### Oppositional Behavior

Six-year-old Billy[6] often refused to mind. He refused to go to bed, refused certain foods, refused to clean up after himself. Since interactions were so negative, Billy and his parents ignored or avoided each other as much as possible.

Billy's parents and a counselor constructed a list of the requests that ordinarily produced the arguing. Then they planned some consequences for his behavior. When poor performance was evident, Billy was sent to his room for ten minutes (time out). If he did as he was asked, his parents praised and commented on his good behavior immediately (differential attention).

The parents arranged 40-minute practice sessions during which they asked him to clean his room, pay attention, finish his meal, etc. During the initial practice sessions no consequences were used. The score for oppositional behavior (guff and refusal) was over 150 per 40-minute session. When they applied the consequences, this behavior approached zero after five sessions.

Five-year-old Sammy was described as "destructive" as well as stubborn. He and his parents just couldn't get along. Tantrums, fights, and an occasional use of "the belt" were typical of the usual day.

As with Billy, Sammy's family began using 40-minute practice sessions with time out and differential attention. The bad behavior dropped from a frequency of over 160 per session to 20 per session in five days. When they stopped using time out and started "attending to" (disciplining) bad behavior in their old way, the parents were saddled with 180 outbursts per 40-minute session again. Reapplying time out and differential attention brought the behavior to nearly zero.

For the love of Billy and Sammy and their families, a little planning did a lot of good.

To remove this consequence and allow the tantrum or other obnoxious behavior to go unrewarded is a courageous decision for any parent to make. The first result of such a tactic is likely to be bigger and better tantrums—especially if a long history of rewarded behavior is being disrupted. When a soft drink machine fails to give a drink for your coin, do you quietly walk away and never put another coin in another machine? No. It is more likely that you will try another coin, kick the machine, bang on its buttons, and then—only then—look for some new behavior that might be successful. So be ready for some desperate behavior when reward is first removed from the tantrum. Also be ready to supply that reward for some new behaviors, for when the child who throws tantrums finally begins to cast about for a new behavior, a new problem develops. He is looking for some new way to get your reward. What will he find? That will be up to the person giving the reward. Parents must plan to reward some other behavior whenever they plan not to reward bad behavior.

## Sins of Omission

If the parent allows the tantrum child to "cry it out," he may find this course unusually trying for the first few tantrums. The child feels that he needs more attention and will continue to look for ways to get it. Removing attention for the tantrum puts more pressure on the child. The tantrum was one of his ways to get his portion of consideration, but it no longer works. Deprivation of attention will be greater than it was in the circumstances that first produced the tantrums. So in this case it is necessary to plan to provide attention for some good behavior while removing it from the bad behavior. A plan to attend some new behaviors should be in effect—a plan developed not on a minute-to-minute basis but on a daily basis.

As an example of this kind of planning about deprivation, consider the case of a fourth-grader who took up to four hours each night to complete his homework. Only about a half-hour's worth of work was assigned, but this child continually prolonged doing his homework. In the behavioral approach, the question "Why?" is here interpreted to mean "What happened next?" What result did the child get when he squirmed, dropped his pencil, made excuses to go to the kitchen or bathroom and returned to find that he had lost the page, asked to call a friend about the assignment, and so forth? It was the prolonged attention of an exasperated mother that happened next. To prove this point the mother was asked, "What would have happened if he had responded in an acceptable way by doing his homework in a short time?" The mother said that she would have been very happy and might have been able to "make dinner on time for a change." If he had done his work well, she would have gone away. If he prolonged the homework, then attention was what happened next.

At first, the solution to this problem may seem to be merely to remove attention for procrastinating homework behavior. But the child is working to get his mother's attention, and it would be wrong simply to remove that reward. Another opportunity for the child to receive her attention must be planned. We cannot remove more attention just because we have found out that he is working for it. The discovery provides a means to select a new activity. In this case, a new strategy was constructed. The new rule was that the child could receive his mother's help with homework from 4:00 to 4:30 each afternoon but could not receive help with the homework after that interval (that is, for procrastinating). It was also decided that if the child finished his homework before dinner, then a half-hour after dinner would be reserved when either his mother or his father would engage in a game or project of the child's choice.

With this strategy in effect, changing the consequences and restricting their effects to a reasonable length of time, homework time dropped from four hours to forty-five minutes. In addition, the mother remained alert to other possible behaviors that deserved her attention. She soon had her son's help in preparing dinner. Merely removing a social consequence from a bad behavior was not the aim of this strategy. More attention was provided somewhere else, and this new attention was given *as a result of designated good behaviors*—the completion of the homework problems and help with the preparation of dinner.

Supposedly, anything that a child ordinarily obtains could be withheld, but our culture guarantees some of the basics. Deprivation of the obvious things is generally infrequent. Food, water, and sleep are easily obtained. Deprivation of attention might be a little more difficult to recognize, for it requires an analysis, similar to the one in the homework example above. Deprivation of general activity can be even more unrecognizable and therefore even more bothersome. A child does not naturally know how to entertain himself or how to find something to do. And it will not suffice to provide gadgetry in his playpen or room and have him play on his own. This type of hit-or-miss situation provides no practice, no consequence.

## EXPERIMENT 6

### Differential Attention

Greg[7] had been kept back in first grade an extra year because of poor academic and social behavior. Edwin, like Greg, was also a problem in class and a slow learner. As a team they were enough to drive an otherwise sane teacher to early retirement.

Observers making judgements of each child every 10 seconds for 30-minute sessions found that the boys attended to class activities only 30% of the time. The teacher was then asked to give differential attention to Edwin when he was paying attention and not fooling around. She was not to change her reactions to Greg at this time. During a second phase of the experiment it was only Greg who received the differential attention. Differential attention meant not only recognizing, praising, and encouraging good behavior, but also completely ignoring bad behavior. In a later phase the teacher gave differential attention to both boys. The graphs in Figure 1 show the improvement.

**FIGURE 1**
Percent of time Edwin and Greg paid attention during experimental sessions.

(Adapted with permission of the **Journal of Applied Behavior Analysis.** Broden, M., Bruce, C., Mitchell, M.A., Carter, V., and Hall, R. V. "Effects of teacher attention on attending behavior of two boys at adjacent desks." **Journal of Applied Behavior Analysis.** 1970, 3, 201. Copyright 1971 by the Society for the Experimental Analysis of Behavior, Inc.)

On the other hand, behaviors learned by rewarded practice provide structuring, direction, and, in the long run, a greater range of learned capabilities to choose from. If some structuring is not provided for the child who is deprived of opportunities for activity, he will cast about in search of such things and over the undirected years come up with some very undesirable habits. How a child entertains himself may be very bothersome if he has no responsibilities to fulfill, no opportunity for enjoyable activities, and no reason to expect any reward.

Do not conclude that you must constantly watch your child to see that he has something to do. The constant watching is of his situation, his opportunities. He need not always be doing something rewarding—all people want to sit and rest sometimes. Some ongoing rewarded responsibilities should be available, however. Some chores, for example, should be assigned and rewarded without specifying exactly when they are to be done. If you have a few jobs that you can do when the mood hits you, then that sudden opportunity or impulse for activity has a greater probability of resulting in a behavior that is approved—and rewarded.

Washing the car, cleaning his room, practicing a musical instrument, working in the yard, and doing some kinds of homework are all examples of responsibilities that could be assigned to a child with a rule that states the reward but does not specify the time that the performance has to be finished. As long as the trumpet is practiced by 8 P.M., the reward will occur. If at all possible, leave the selection of the exact time to the child, thus removing nagging and badgering and at the same time allowing the child a little more freedom in the selection of a routine.

What if he procrastinates and the behavior does not occur? What if he keeps on missing practice by letting the time go by? Then the reward is not being used, and it is time to look for a better one. In some cases, it may also be time to ask yourself if you are demanding too much for these first rewards.

## *The Pursuit of "Perfection"*

If the behavioral approach outlined in this book is taken, how can you be sure anything has changed in the mind of the child? Regardless of your approach to child rearing, this question will remain partially unanswered. The only way that one can know anything about another person is through the way that person acts and speaks. The person's internal states will have to be inferred from those behaviors. Thus, we can never be sure of a "cure" as that word is ordinarily used.

The idea of a cure also implies that some general change has taken place in the individual. And if you use the approach described here, it is impossible to provide well-thought-out consequences and programs of learning for *all* the possible behaviors that a child can go through. You can focus on only one or two behavioral problems at a time, contrive the consequences for those, and carry them out. For all other behaviors, you must continue to rely on the ordinary sequence of events. Nor can you use the word "cure" in the sense of a permanent change; there is never a guarantee that some unforeseen circumstance will not develop in which the consequences are changed. You could not hope to control all the consequences and combinations of consequences that might have the potential of changing behavior.

The procedures described in this book focus on individual behavioral problems. The changes in behavior brought about by these procedures will be relatively permanent and that permanency can be somewhat ensured by carefully selecting behaviors that you, the parents, know are likely to be supported by social rewards from you and others. For that you will have to rely on your ability to learn to observe what result—what consequence, what reward—follows the individual activities that are of interest to you. You will have to learn to narrow your observations and to focus your efforts on small problems for extended periods of time. The repetition of consequences is the basic rule. Practice implies repetition and, in the context of this book, repetition of consequences. Bold strokes that suddenly get through to the child are seldom accomplished. It is what he has come to expect as a result of his consistent experiences that determines his behavior patterns.

## OBJECTIVES  *chapter two*

1. Explain the importance of allowing children to make some of their own decisions and experience the consequences of those decisions.

2. List some conclusions that might apply to "behaviors of concern".

3. What are the disadvantages of a consequence such as: "If you are not nice today you will not go to the circus on Saturday."?

4. Give an example of a consequence that is repeatable.

5. What is the most effective reward used in the home?

6. Why is reward generally favorable to punishment?

7. List two ways in which the family disposition can be modified.

8. The disposition to set unrealistic and ill-defined standards of behavior is usually due to what?

9. Summarize the likely results of a planning session by parents.

10. What is the most obvious characteristic of "bad disposition" behavior?

11. What are two disadvantages of punishment?

12. List two advantages of keeping a chart of observations of behavior.

13. Give an example of the rule that consequences must be judged by how they effect behavior, not by what parents think their effect should be.

14. What are two advantages of assigning chores to your children without putting exact time limits on them?

# 3 / Understanding Behavior

**E**very person likes to feel that his activities are useful and important. This is just as true of a child as it is of an adult. A child's continual retort, "Why?" when requested to do something, may be partly an attention-getting device, but it is also a search for a reason. When he asks for "the reason" he has to do something he usually wants a reward but he also needs justification. No one likes to be forced, tempted, or even encouraged to do something that seems to be of no value. The best way to convince a person that an activity is worthwhile is to show him that the activity pays off in a useful way.

## In Search of Meaning

The dropout who finds school of no use is a child who has been requested to perform in ways that *for him* have no importance (rewards, results, or accomplishments). Adults see the meaningfulness and importance of getting a good education, but in many cases it is not enough to say to a child, "You can't get anywhere without a good education." The parent means that if the child does not have a good education, jobs will be harder to get, he may not be promoted, and—as a result—he may not be able to buy some of the things he wants. But, at the moment, the youth does not want all those things. He may be able to get a job that for him pays well. He does not care about the future or job security. The "getting anywhere" idea is not meaningful to him. The consequences are too far in the future and too abstract for him. A small amount of money in his pocket now is enough, and he does not need much education to get that.

So why should a child study decimals in the fifth and sixth grades? Of what use is it to know portions of American history? Why are spelling lists so important? Realistic activities must be provided for him that will demonstrate why these tools are important. As the child learns new things at school each day, he must be encouraged to use that knowledge and skill each day at home. If he is encouraged, the usefulness of learning becomes part of the reward. Why not allow a child to use his decimals in keeping track of the family checking account? Why not leave notes concerning a telephone call for a child of seven to read as you would for an adult? Why not provide opportunities for a child to write letters concerning family business or to write letters other than thank-you notes to relatives? There are many activities in a family situation that could show, in a concrete way, the usefulness and importance of skills learned in school.

The way such skills can be applied has been shown by one mother who takes her son to the bank and allows him to go in alone and pay the bills. If he comes back with the exact change and correctly explains the arithmetic to her, she gives him 15 cents of the change. He will never ask why he has to study arithmetic. He knows. His younger sister is allowed to bake for her mother. When recipes are to be cut in half or doubled, the mother does not interfere with the calculations. From bitter (and sour) experience this child too knows why arithmetic is important.

It is also necessary for a child to learn about the importance of skills that are not learned in school. Cooking, washing the car, sewing, and repairing domestic items are things most of us have to do all our lives. Allowing a child to practice these things early, with support from the parent for successes, will help him not only to face these tasks later but also to learn something productive now.

What activity can your child do now — on his own — which is useful and productive? The graph below emphasizes one way a child might grow up. It is also a way to measure the success of the parents because it keeps track of the useful activities a child does for himself. Notice that it doesn't count what he *can do* if put to the test. The graph counts what he *does* as his own responsibility *day to day*.

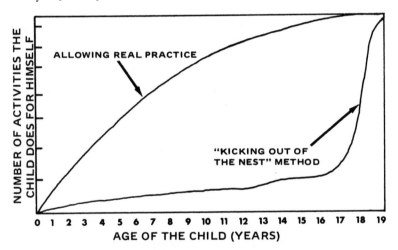

Don't feel discouraged if your child requires a little praise, recognition, or even the concrete incentive of allowance money. All of us need something of that type to keep going. The major question is are you allowing your children to practice their behavior in these early years and gradually expanding the kinds of practice? Or, are you making their phone calls, their beds, their lunches; getting his toothbrush, her homework materials, their bank accounts; arranging his ride to school, dentist appointment, summer camp; and picking up her toys, clothes, gerbil, black beetle, and mushed peanut butter sandwich? Are you still telling him when to go to bed, get up, what to wear, what to play, when to play it, with whom, and how long?

The home is such a nice protected place to fade out all of this control and dependency. You're there to see that the consequences of real practice are not allowed to hurt too much. You're there to backtrack and help again for a while if your child has tried some responsibility too soon or too fast. Give responsibility now, gradually, not abruptly on the steps of a college dormitory, or in the back of a church just before a ceremony. By then you've missed your chance to help with the learning. Only birds fly when abruptly kicked out of the nest. Humans need to be better prepared and more experienced.

Because such learning is itself rewarding, use this knowledge

---

## EXPERIMENT 7

### Token Reward in the Home

**Family One:** George (age nine), Dollie (age eight), and Keith (age five)[8] all contributed minor problems to the family. George was sassy and skipped school occasionally. Dollie was hyperactive and threw tantrums. Keith whined a lot. While there was no need for intense concern about these behaviors, no "growing up" was occurring, and the family atmosphere was not very pleasant.

With the help of a counselor, behaviors were selected and defined. Chores, bedtime behavior, whining, and bickering were selected as the first targets. They were defined as follows:

Make beds: When you make the bed, sheets and blankets should be tucked in, no big wrinkles, pillow at head, stuffed animals arranged neatly.

Bedtime: At bedtime, no talking, laughing, verbal or physical interaction after five minutes.

Whining: Complaints in a high wavering voice will be considered whining.

Bickering: Loud arguing between the children is bickering.

Points were awarded or subtracted when

as a means of calming your impatience. The parent must learn to tolerate the inconvenience of allowing a child to do some of the important things. For some activities, mistakes are easy to tolerate and rewards are easy to give because the parent and the child know how important it is to learn the activities. Now, remember one more rule: move over a little as your child grows into your world. Don't insist that he or she fit just the niche that you wish.

If you get too picky about *how* he picks up his clothes, *how* she brushes her teeth, *what* colors he wears together, you're going to be a nagging, picky person. The situation will be basically a punishing one and *everyone* (you and your spouse included) will want out.

Begin early, be tolerant, and start with easy things but don't stick with child's play too long. Child's play is, of course, necessary even for adults. But, as adults know so well, to have mere child's

the children behaved correctly or incorrectly.

The parents then wrote down the points earned each day on cards. These points could be exchanged for basic privileges for the children the following day, and for special treats when extra points accumulated.

Within five weeks chores were performed reliably every day. With the addition of fines, bickering, teasing, and whining were reduced from the initial six-to-ten times a day to one or two times a day.

**Family Two:** Teresa was ten and her brother, Robin, was seven. They hated doing everyday chores. Rather than nagging, their parents checked off chores completed each day on a sheet of paper. All chores were defined and inspected at 9 p.m. every day.

The parents tried giving feedback for good performance — leaving a copy of the day's results in the child's room. Behavior remained poor. Then they added gold stars but with little effect. Giving ten cents per chore improved things somewhat! And, when they added a 58-cent bonus for completing all daily chores the results were just short of perfect.

play continually pushed upon you is annoying and insulting. Children feel that way too. To a one-year-old all activities are of some interest and value, but as he grows up the distinction between play and work becomes more clear and important. To a five-year-old, playing with his father is a big thing. But a ten- or twelve-year-old wants to know the importance of or reason for doing jobs or playing games — which may explain a common parental complaint: "He always wants to know what's in it for him — he's so selfish."

It is not always the *concrete* payoff that the child is acting selfish about. Many times his question is meant to be more general. What's in it for anyone? Of what importance would this activity be to anyone? What respect from others will be obtained by doing it? What feeling of accomplishment could be obtained by doing it?

Many things in life that have to be done are drudgery. Such activities may be very dull and may seem to be of little importance. Nor does a person gain respect from others for such jobs. There may be no result to be proud of. When a parent asks a child to do such drudgery, a great deal of encouragement is needed to show the child that the activity is worth doing. So the child's question "Why should I do this?" is important because it shows he needs appreciation for doing this job. For activities that are not very important, fun, or adult, he's counting on you for support. His question about drudgery is a signal to focus on encouraging him to do the job and praising him for doing it.

## Definitions for Action

To know when to give a reward as a consequence for a behavior, a clear description of the behavior is necessary so that you will know it when you see it. You might, for example, make a bet concerning which of two children will pleasantly share his toys with a stranger, but how will you decide what conditions determine a winner? A more precise definition of "sharing" is needed. To bet on the behavior of a horse in a race is easy because everyone agrees on the behavioral definition of a winner, but to bet on the behavior of a child engaged in something other than a race may be a difficult problem.

A concrete and objective definition of "sharing," as well as some agreed-upon observable actions, must be established to avoid a disagreement between the bettors. Otherwise, there is too much margin for misinterpretation; the bettors will not know how to react. Perhaps it could be decided that if a child offers one of his toys to or allows it to be handled by another child, that will be called sharing. For the purposes of the bet, it is not necessary to know why the child shares one of his toys. He may share it because someone is watching, or he may share it "for the wrong reasons" (to con the other child out of one of his possessions, for example). Obviously, characteristics of the child's approach to the situation are not being taken into account by this definition. But it does emphasize the level of behavioral description necessary to get two people to agree on what a third person is doing. Thus, if parents are to agree and to provide a unified front with a consistent and prompt reaction to a given behavior, this kind of behavioral description will be necessary.

Behavioral definitions help parents agree on when to reward the child. This decision is important. If the parents have agreed on what the good behavior is, then the good behavior is a signal to give reward. The behavioral definition thus helps plan the timing of rewards. It acts as a cue for when to give or to withhold reward.

For the purposes of the bet, the behavioral definition of sharing was one child's offering or allowing another child to handle one of his toys. The act of sharing would be the signal to reward the child with social attention and approval. The act of snatching a toy from his playmate or of not sharing it would be a signal to withhold social attention and approval. The temptation to correct or reprimand the child for this error deserves careful consideration. If he is reprimanded, he will receive social attention. It might be that, as in a tantrum, any social attention is a reward, so you cannot allow yourself the luxury of reprimands. The behavioral definition will help police your reactions. It will provide the cue.

In addition to making things clear for the parents, a rule about a clearly defined behavior will allow the child to understand quickly what he is to do and why he is to do it. Furthermore, the consistency of the parents' reaction will have to be clear. The child may become confused when either the behavior or the reaction is too vague and variable. Little talks will not clear up this problem; only consistent and repeated practice with reasonable, precisely stated rules will have a durable effect.

As a matter of fact, it is not always essential that all the whys and wherefores concerning the results of the child's behavior be pointed out verbally; none of us completely understands all that. If a child requests more explanation than you have given, then he should be given all the explanation that is possible. But what is important for learning and for producing reliable and desirable behavior is a consistent relationship between the events themselves. When you learn to drive a car, you need not comprehend the mechanisms of the engine. As long as the accelerator, brake, steering wheel, and key consistently result in the functioning of the car, you can learn and perform reliably. It is not necessary to have the understanding of an engineer and the insight of a mechanic. What is essential for learning to drive a car is that the car react reliably. In the same way, a child gains experience with a reliable set of rules without knowing all the mechanisms that result in a given behavior producing a given result, and most behaviors are learned without a complete understanding of the mechanisms by which they are effective.

It would be a waste of time for every driving school to give a course on internal-combustion engines, and it may be a waste of time to tell a child continually why he must wash his hands before meals. A long and repeated explanation may even be rewarding attention for dirty hands. Some learning must go forward without repeated explanations. Understanding the mechanisms will have to wait. A study concerning this understanding of mechanisms that is basic to the history of behaviorism was conducted by E. R. Guthrie and G. P. Horton.

In their experiments, a cat was placed in a problem box. As most cat owners will tell you, it is not in a cat's make-up to be content while confined in a small place. In the center of the box was a pole that, if pushed by the cat, would open a door and allow its escape. But because the cat did not know that, it tried various kinds of activities that might be solutions to its imprisonment. It mewed. It cried. It scratched the walls. But none of these activities related to pushing the pole, and it did not escape. Eventually, in pacing around, the cat bumped the pole accidentally and gained freedom. The cat's discovery was not an insight any more than a child's first successful use of a doorknob is an insight. It was an accident. Nevertheless, a certain behavior resulted in a certain consequence, and the probability that the behavior would again occur was increased because it was successful in obtaining a desired result. On most occasions, the cat released the latch by rubbing the pole in the same manner as a cat rubbing a person's leg. The cat had not "learned" that the pole was attached to a spring that operated a latch that would release the door. It knew nothing about mechanical engineering. Rather, it learned to stand in a certain place, rub a pole, and thus obtain its release. Is it necessary to talk about what was happening inside the cat to describe the process going on? Did the cat "understand" the box? Obviously, the answer to these questions is "No," yet one can still easily describe what the cat was doing and why.

Most of the everyday behaviors learned by human beings are learned through such processes as the one just described. Most people do not understand the events that take place when they turn a key in the family car. Like the cat, they understand only that certain activities produce certain results. Isn't that, at times, enough?

## Balancing Acts

The process of specifying behaviors and consequences and changing the consequences is the development of a strategy. The word "strategy" may at first imply a little too much struggling, a little too much confrontation, or even scheming. And there is a little of each of these in child rearing. The important thing is that you devote some time each week to conscious, routine planning. Consider how much time and energy children devote to figuring out how to accomplish *their* goals. When parents neglect the planning, a scheming child can win every round. How common this situation is became evident when parents in a training group were asked to spend fifteen to thirty minutes each week in a strategy session. Most parents found it difficult to set aside even this much time. On the other hand, their children, without jobs and domestic responsibilities, continued to spend a great portion of their time trying out new ideas and methods on their parents.

This statement is not meant to imply that all children are scheming little devils, but they do constantly experiment with and experience their family situations. If the parents of a fifteen-year-old wonder why they seem to have lost control over their son, they might consider how many hours of the past few years he spent struggling with his adjustments to his position in the family compared with the number of hours they spent thinking through some plans for change. Most parents of "children gone wrong" have not made bad decisions that led to bad procedures; rather, they have made little conscious effort to reach *any* objective decision, and *that*, in turn, led to bad procedures.

Thus, the strategy session is a necessity. It allows parents to regroup, to compromise, and to agree on a united front. The session ensures that consequences will be consistent and applied immediately. It need not be secretive. In almost all cases it is beneficial to report, in an informal way, the results of the strategy session to the children. If a strategy will work only as long as the children do not find out about it, then it is dishonest and probably unrealistic, because the children will find out anyway.

The questions that should be discussed in the strategy sessions include: What's wrong (*complaints*)? What do we have now and what do we want to have (*definitions*)? What usually happens next and what could be used as incentive (*consequences*)? A final question, how we can design the practice, will be discussed in Chapter 6.

COMPLAINTS / It is worth the trouble to write down a complaint so that it is related to a specific understandable characteristic of the child. It is also worthwhile to state why, in your view, the behavior should be changed. List the reasons. List also other good and bad things about this child.

Diverting your attention to other behaviors of the child for a moment is helpful in deciding how important your complaint is in relation to his general behavior. When this broad view is considered, the complaint may not get at the problem. If so, you will have to restate it.

Your complaint might be too trivial, too unimportant to worry about. The behavior does not have to be the most important problem to merit attention, but perhaps it is too far down the list. If so, do not consider the exercise a waste of time. Some positive action should come from this decision, for you will no longer be preoccupied with a problem that you have decided is too trivial to worry about. Inhibit the next correction, the next reprimand for that behavior. Let it go! You decided it was not important. As you put this decision into practice, there will be another advantage. The behavior will cause you less agitation, because you have decided it is not important enough to worry about. The family will be happier, because you have fewer complaints. Your decision that drinking the last half-inch of milk in the glass is not important and will now be ignored makes dinner more pleasant for everyone.

But suppose the complaint is not trivial, and you need to do something about it.

DEFINITIONS  /  The first and most important point is to focus upon the behaviors, the particular activities, that seem to be of concern. The activities are of concern either because they are bad ones that are happening or because they are good ones that are not happening. For example, a parent might complain that a child is not neat. Neatness is not something that happens in a discrete manner. One cannot easily point out exactly when the child is being neat and when he is not; neatness is a general characteristic, and the times for giving and withholding consequences will be hard to determine. A step from the complaint toward the behavioral definition is needed: he does not comb his hair; he does not pick up his toys and clothes; he does not tie his shoes. Or, if the problem is that the child is flippant or boisterous or aggressive, the definition might be: he makes a smart remark when corrected; he talks loudly at meals; or he hits other children. *What, in fact, does he do that you don't like?* This clarification will make it much easier to begin some analysis of what happens next when the child performs in these ways.

Behavioral definitions have three goals: (1) to state the specific nature of the problem, (2) to help specify the nature of consequences, and (3) to guide the search for the simplest behavior that can first be rewarded. The child must be able to perform the behavior easily. This level of behavior must be far enough back—low enough, if you will—to ensure that many opportunities for reward will be available on the first day the rule is used. The selection of this level must be carefully thought out. It is a very important selection. If the first behavior is not easy and simple, there will be few opportunities for reward and the system will not have been tested.

It is tempting to set out a "reasonable demand" for performance. The difficulty with such a demand is that it indicates what the parents think the child should be. Of primary interest is a behavioral level that takes into account the child's present level. After things are going well, you can worry about the successive steps necessary to lead him to where he should be.

To use consequences to obtain behaviors, a beginning must be made by rewarding something that is *already* being performed. Long-range hopes for the future cannot be rewarded; they can suggest only what present behavior can be strengthened to start you on your way. The behaviors you plan for are not here, and you cannot wait for them to happen accidentally. You will not even be able to wait for improvement; you must start rewarding what you have. So plan to reward some behavior on the first day. To state the principle with its correct emphasis: "By giving rewards, you want to strengthen a behavior." The reverse of this statement is true, but it has the wrong emphasis for the first steps: "You want to strengthen behavior by giving rewards." First comes a reward for an expected behavior and then, after practice, a change, a strengthening, of behavior. Once a behavior has been strengthened in this way, the little steps in the right direction can be rewarded.

For example, if your child comes home with a failure on a spelling test, your temptation may be to drill him on the errors he has made. Although that is the ultimate goal, it ensures that the frequency of early rewards will be low and the frequency of early failures will be high. First ask the child for some earlier list of words that you know he will get right—the list from two weeks ago. Run through that list first, noting with pride and encouragement all his successes. Next, try later ones until he is ready, encouraged by recent success, to tackle the new list. Begin, of course, with the words he got right and then mix in the harder ones. Your plan must ensure that the behavior will pay off from the beginning.

Another example of starting back far enough involves the

extreme behavior problem in the school. The student, frequently a boy, cannot sit still, keep his attention on his work, or stay out of trouble with other students. The promise of some long-term consequence (grades, threats of failing) has no effect on him. In

## EXPERIMENT 8

### Arranging the World
### For Good Behavior

Eight fat people[9] responded to an ad for a weight control experiment. After checking with their doctors they were asked to sign a contract which said that they would give up certain valued possessions (money, trophies, medals, clothes, jewelry) if they didn't lose weight according to the schedule described in the contract.

The pudgy subjects deposited their valuables with the experimenter and gained them back only when they: 1) lost two pounds, or 2) reduced to the specified weight level for that week, and 3) reached the final weight level by their deadline.

From time to time the experimenter "temporarily called off" the experiment. The weight loss always reversed and the scales went up. However, over a 200-to-400-day period, the subjects lost up to 40 pounds.

Eight hospital staff members[10] volunteered to wear a simple shoulder harness. When the harness was stretched by slouching, it turned on a little buzzer

placed against their shoulder blades. Although the buzzer could only be felt and not heard, and was not at all painful, slouching decreased from 58% of the time to 10% of the time. And later, even with the feedback device removed, the subjects slouched only 35% of the time.

Three cigarette smokers[11] completed an experiment to reduce their habit. Each time the smoker opened his cigarette case an electric shock was delivered to his arm. Smokers reduced the number of cigarettes they smoked as the intensity of the shock was increased by the experimenter. However, the experiment began with 20 smokers!

Twenty-nine-thousand students[12] could use the campus bus at a large university. Nevertheless, the average number of riders per day was only about 300. A new kind of bus token was given to the riders intermittently. This token was free and could be exchanged for ice cream, cheeseburgers, coffee, etc. as well as for further rides. The number of daily riders rose to nearly 500!

light of the previous discussion, it is tempting to focus on some aspect of this general problem by using a precise behavioral definition—and try to build up his sitting in his seat, then get his attention, then work on his fighting troubles. But these behaviors seem to be so interrelated that they must all be dealt with at one time. When this is the situation, consider cutting down on the first level to be rewarded. Concentrate on all three behaviors at the same time, but only for a short period. Require changes in all three behaviors right away: the student should sit in his seat, be quiet, and pay attention, but reward should come after a very short period of time.

The overall amount of good behavior demanded is reduced in the sense that you have asked that all good behavior last for only a short duration of time rather than that one part of it last for a long time. Because it is difficult for you, the parents, to reward immediately behaviors that occur in the classroom, a very useful system is the so-called token economy, in which a desired behavior is rewarded immediately by a plastic token or a ticket, which the student can later exchange for a previously determined (and mutually understood) reward, such as extra play time or some other privilege. In this particular situation, the system might be explained to the student this way: "If you stay in your seat *and* work for the first ten minutes of the class, the teacher will give you a ticket signed by your mother that will allow you to play outside for half an hour when you come home from school." That's all the opportunity for outside play there is the first week; the rest of the time he stays inside. During the second week there are two tickets available for each of two ten-minute work periods. When the tickets have reached the maximum number (say four, if two hours of after-school play are usually allowed), then you may start increasing the "price" of the tickets. Now he gets two hours of play for forty minutes of work in class (four tickets). The next step requires fifteen minutes of work for each ticket so that the total work requirement is increased to an hour.

You do not want to increase the teacher's work in this situation, and you do not want the child to get a great deal of direct attention concerned with either his bad behavior or the system being used to deal with it. Therefore, the teacher must be asked to refrain from discussing the behavior in class. The child either does or does not get the card. There should be no arguments, no repeated explanations, and no threats.

There are three important points of caution here. First, the teacher must be consistent and keep in mind a behavioral definition of what ten minutes of "work" is. Second, the mother must also play the game strictly. Third, the child must understand from the beginning that the rules will change along the way.

In some cases you may have to ask yourself one more question about your behavioral definition: "Is it concerned with a behavior I want changed or is it really concerned with talking about that behavior?" It is easy for a parent to become concerned about what a child or teen-ager *says* he is going to do. The real concern should be about what he *does*. Consider, for example, a child who continually makes rude remarks about his teacher. Such remarks always elicit a sharp reprimand from his parents and provide an exchange with them that is challenging and entertaining to the child. Of course, the child may have no intention of saying these things in school; they are purely for exciting engagements at home. If the parents want to change this behavior because it is annoying, there is an obvious way to do it: ignore the behavior, or comment in a calm and matter-of-fact way without providing the usual fight. If the child actually makes remarks against his teacher at school, however, the parents want to change the school behavior. They must not be distracted from that job by a talking behavior at home.

Parents often spend time and effort getting children to agree with them, that is, to *say* that they agree with them. This situation is usually distasteful to everyone, and the effort might be better spent organizing consequences for the good and bad behaviors instead of talking about agreement. Have long talks with your child by all means, but do not make life unpleasant by continually trying to change a verbal behavior (the way he talks about this or that). Perhaps your real concern should be not the way he talks about the behavior but the way he performs it. It makes no sense to argue a child into saying he will try harder in school. Arguing takes the place of planning a change, and parents need that time and energy to plan. Planning can ensure a reason for the child to try harder.

## OBJECTIVES   *chapter three*

1.  Why is it a good idea to provide the
    child with realistic activities, such
    as balancing a check book, or pay-
    ing bills?

2.  List three advantages of using be-
    havioral definitions when trying to
    change a child's behavior.

3.  What are some of the functions of a
    planning session?

4.  What are the three goals of behavioral
    definitions?

5.  What is the difference between be-
    havior and talking about behavior?

# 4 / Facing the Consequences

The important goal of child rearing is the development of adult behaviors supported and maintained by adult consequences. So before searching for special consequences for children, it's best to ask about consequences for adults. These consequences that guide our behavior will, in the long run, be the consequences available to our children.

Applying the more logical adult consequences would be most realistic considering our long range goal. For example, if a child continually disrupts dinner with loud, inappropriate comments and giggling, you might ask, "What would we do if he were an adult at our table, say, a visitor—Uncle George perhaps?" You might first try to change the subject and calm him down by talking about something of interest to him. If that did not work, you would probably tell him off. And if that did not work, you would probably no longer tolerate his behavior. He would have to eat elsewhere. Possibly a child should be treated in the same way. You might start by trying to change the subject of the dinner conversation to one that would be of interest to the child. If that doesn't work, the child could eat earlier or later than the parents for a while, then be given another chance to eat with them.

Related to the selection of logical consequences is the question of logical behaviors. Bad behavior may merely be the alternative to good (logical) behavior because the good behavior doesn't pay off. After we question logical *consequences* we must question the opportunity for good *behavior*. If the child were not participating in a particular bad behavior, what behavior would be available for him and what would happen if he did it? Often, bad behavior appears because there is no suggestion for, or incentive for, any *particular* good behavior. When father sits down to dinner, he has all the stories of his day to tell. Mother wants to report on the activities of her day. Their conversation is punctuated by, "Sit up on your chair," "Eat your peas," "Don't spill your milk," "Drink your milk," and so on. How does the child get his share of the attention in this adult dinner conversation? By acting badly. What attention would he get if he did not participate in this bad behavior? None. Of course, the conversation at dinner should be partly at the child's level, and, he should also receive attention for good behaviors.

Attention would also be the consequence for the child whose behavior becomes a problem during lulls in classroom activities. The problem is maintained not only because attention is given to bad behavior but because no attention is given to good behavior. One might say that the child does not know enough to busy himself during these times. But it is probably more accurate to say that the opportunities for good behaviors are not obvious enough to him. He cannot be expected to know what to do. With his lack of practice, he has no reason to expect benefits from worthwhile activities, and the few times he tried it the behavior did not pay off. In this case, a lack of consequences for good behaviors has brought about the problem, in addition to the support for bad behavior. Of course, there are other factors such as the attention and support from peers for bad behavior in a classroom, but those aspects of the classroom situation are unchangeable. It is best, therefore, to reexamine the opportunity for other behaviors and their rewards. More frequent praise and attention for work would help point out proper ways to get attention and would reduce some of the hunger for attention.

## Focusing on Good Behavior

Too often the behavioral approach deals with things we would like to get rid of. The majority of parents' complaints are about bad behaviors that they wish were not there. Complaints about good behaviors that are missing are not nearly as common. It is easy to complain that a child is in his room all the time. But when he comes out of his room, what awaits him? What consequence will occur and for what behaviors? In many cases this question cannot be answered precisely enough to convince anyone to come from anywhere. An effort must be made to make incentives for and opportunities for behaviors out of the child's room.

Be careful when you try to arrange consequences for "non-behaviors." Be careful when using rules that say, "If you don't do such and such [watch TV, walk on the flowers in the yard, and so on], I will reward you." A nonbehavior does not happen at a particular time, so the time to give reward will be rather arbitrary. The nonbehavior rule fails to specify an *obvious* time for reward. It also fails to specify what the child *should* do. A positive rule would be better. For example, when dealing with a child who is too possessive and refuses to share his things, it may be pertinent for you to understand that he receives more attention when he refuses to share than when he does not. If he did not act possessive when company came, how would he be rewarded? State this answer as a rule about behavior, not as a rule about a nonbehavior.

The complaint that a child watches too much TV involves the same problem. Usually no alternative has been suggested. Certainly no consequence has been prepared for such an event. Most parents would be at a loss to keep the child busy if he did come out of his room or away from the TV. Constructing a new situation to change some of these problems involves more than merely changing consequences. It involves discovering new behaviors that will be rewarded.

Does this mean that you must go out and buy bigger and better toys? Probably not. Most parents have found new toys to be very temporary distractions.

## EXPERIMENT 9

### Selective Reward

Three-year-old Sara[13] sucked her thumb while holding her blanket. Before naptime each day, the experimenter at the day-care center would read to her for 20 minutes. Each time Sara sucked her thumb the therapist would immediately stop reading and just stare at the page. The graph in Figure 2 shows the success of this peculiarly selective "on and off" reading on Sara's behavior. It's important to note that during the "off" times Sara hit the therapist. In addition, her mother reported "no improvement at home." Nevertheless, "contingent reading" lowered thumbsucking to zero for as long as the therapist could stand it.

Rosie was six and sucked her thumb while holding soft objects and watching television. Rosie's mother followed the same reading procedure (she stopped reading and stared at the book when thumbsucking was occurring). Rosie showed improvement both during and outside of these sessions. Rosie caught on, saying, "I know why you're not reading." But the procedure worked anyway.

The same procedure was tried on eight-year-old Jennifer who held a blanket and sucked her thumb while lying in bed. However, she made an adjustment to the times when the reading was discontinued. She pulled down her own reading material from a nearby shelf and continued sucking! With the bed moved away from the shelf thumbsucking went to zero in order for the reading to continue. Since her mother was the experimenter, thumbsucking ceased in other situations where she was present as well.

A fifth-grade teacher[14] removed five boys from class for 15-minute reading sessions each day. She rewarded their reading and ignored their disruptive behavior. The disruptions took up about 35% of the time in the first few sessions. When tokens (which could be exchanged for access to a game room, recess, movies, ditto machine, bulletin board, etc.) were given **for good reading only,** the boys' reading performance doubled and disruptions were eliminated.

At the beginning of Chapter 3 the selection of meaningful behaviors was discussed. Apply this principle when you search for alternatives to bad behaviors. Look around for something useful for your child to do—in this case, even drudgery. How about dusting, waxing, painting, setting the table, preparing his own decorations for some party, writing letters, cleaning his

**FIGURE 2**

Percent of time Sara spent thumbsucking as sessions increased.

(Adapted with permission of the **Journal of Applied Behavior Analysis.** Knight, M.F., and McKenzie, H.S. "Elimination of bedtime thumbsucking in home settings through contingent reading." **Journal of Applied Behavior Analysis.** 1974, 7, 36. Copyright 1974 by the Society for the Experimental Analysis of Behavior, Inc.)

room, making up grocery lists, or sweeping floors? "But he won't do it right!" you say. "He'll mess it up!" Of course, it is probably always true that doing a task yourself is the only way to have it done right. However, the purpose of the job is to take the child away from TV or out of his room. The point is not to have the behavior done right but to have the child do the job rather than something else so that he gains practice in doing something useful. But don't forget to plan the consequences. Your time and positive attention or some concrete reward, or both, will have to be there.

## Social Incentives

The stress on consequences does not mean that you should carry around a bag of candy or money to keep your children shaped up. Social rewards of honest appreciation, praise, and encouragement are very effective. Most parents, however, do not stick to the rule of reward when they use social rewards. Be careful about social rewards given for the wrong thing or at the wrong time. Not all reactions to your child should be planned, but some should. A mother who reacts to every little cough or physical complaint of her child on the days following an illness is supporting a behavior just as surely as when she pats him on the head for making his bed. Social rewards are so easy to give that they are used in a very offhand manner—sometimes forgotten when they are most needed, at other times thrown in where they build in the wrong direction.

So your supports, agreements, and encouragements deserve close attention at times. You can't police yourself, watching every move you make and every word you say when you are around your children, and it would be an awful and inhuman situation for anyone who did. But when you consider a specific behavior of your child, always consider the role that your attention plays—for good or ill.

Sophisticated adults give social attention and approval in subtle ways. They use a nod of the head or a lift of the eyebrow or a curiously phrased remark such as "I should think so" or "You bet" or "Oh, really?" Adults have had much practice in using and hearing such subtleties and react to and learn from them. As a child grows up, he learns the value of these things and the information they convey. But the young child has not learned this lesson. Make sure your sophistication does not get in the way when you are trying to give support to a young child who has just performed well. Be frank and outspoken when you like what he has done. Say it straight out in simple language, "Yes, that's good. That's what I like you to do." Say it loudly; say it simply; let him know you mean it.

## A Price Tag on Behavior

Some behaviors may have become so habitual and their solutions so complex that other less natural rewards will have to be selected and given for the very small steps in progress. But you must be sure you are willing to carry out the application of these consequences. For example, to improve the homework study habit, you might make the weekly allowance the consequence. Are you prepared to allow no money at all if your child does not become successful? Probably you will give in somewhere along the way and provide a minimum amount of money. At the other extreme, you are probably not prepared to give any amount of money that the child may suddenly earn by a burst of activity. So it will be better to set limits at the beginning—say, a 25-cent minimum and a 75-cent maximum, or whatever you think is appropriate. You can then guarantee your child a minimum by saying, "You will get an allowance of 25 cents, but you may get as much as 75 cents if you do your workbook assignments. For every page of the workbook you do, I will increase your allowance by 5 cents—up to 75 cents."

With this amount of structure, you will not be forced into an ogrelike position (no allowance) by the bad behavior of your child, and you will not be forced into unreasonable extravagances by bursts of good activity. As the weeks go by, you may demand more assignments for each nickel or you may begin to ask for completion of other spelling and arithmetic assignments. Just be sure the increments are small enough. Remember that you should not demand too much at first or increase the demand too rapidly. If you suddenly demand performance of half-hours or hours of homework from a child who has not stuck with it for 10 minutes

## EXPERIMENT 10

### Positives vs. Negatives

Twelve average families[15] volunteered to participate in an experiment for a week to see if they could present the good side or the bad side of their children when they wanted to. Observers were sent to the homes to count behaviors of both children and parents. The observers were not aware of the instructions given the parents to try to "feel out the observers".

Six of the families were asked to present the "good picture" on the first, third, and fifth nights of observation while the other six families were to present the "good picture" on the second, fourth, and sixth nights. The alternate nights were to be used by each family to present the "bad picture".

Observers arrived for a 45-minute session held just before dinner each evening. Sometimes two observers were used as a check to see that observations were reliable. Observers counted: 1) deviant behaviors of the children (whining, tan-

trums, teasing, destructive behaviors, etc.), 2) positive, negative and neutral responses of the parents, and 3) parental commands. Figure 3 shows how many of each of these were counted for "good" and "bad" days.

The data in Figure 3 verify the parents' own view of how to control children. They reported that they had been more negative, restrictive and disapproving in order to get bad behavior. They became positive, attentive and talkative in order to get the good behavior.

When asked for specifics they said that on bad days they: gave commands and restricted activities; tried to express disapproval and yelled; ignored the child; used slapping and spanking; teased, shamed, or embarrassed the child; and were generally more negative.

When asked how they got the good behavior they said they: paid attention to the child; were positive to the child physically; expressed verbal approval of the child's activity; did what the child asked; talked with him; and were generally more positive.

in a great many months, the frustrations and the probability of failure will be high.

On the other hand, if you begin by asking for some bit of behavior that is so small that it is almost certain to be successful and you give rewards for it, progress can be made. For example, you might merely ask that one page of a workbook assignment be completed before providing a rather large reward such as a

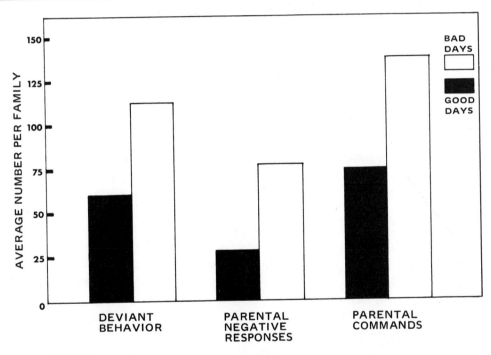

**FIGURE 3**

Average number of "good days" and "bad days" under different parental reactions.

(Adapted with permission of the **Journal of Applied Behavior Analysis.** Johnson, S.M., and Lebitz, G.K. "Parental manipulation of child behavior in home observations." **Journal of Applied Behavior Analysis.** 1974, 7, 28. Copyright, 1974 by the Society for the Experimental Analysis of Behavior, Inc.)

half-hour of TV or possibly some money. In this case the reward is so big and the demand so small that the possibilities of success are very great. Then in a predetermined and announced progression you might ask that more and more workbook pages be completed before you give the reward. When you set up such a rule, be careful that the increments in the demands are small enough to allow a smooth and easy increase in effort on the part of the child.

You must also be careful when selecting this "less logical" reward because it is not one of the natural benefits that you would hope the child would gain from such behaviors. The time will come when these rewards will have to be withdrawn, so the other more social rewards will also have to be emphasized continually. It is not necessary to attempt to phase out such consequences just because they are unnatural; 50 cents a week may be a small price to pay for maintaining the behavior. Eventually, however, the more natural rewards will have to suffice. Thus, the behaviors should be selected for their long-range importance and usefulness, that is, the likelihood that they will be supported by people outside the family.

The activities other people support and believe important are probably the same ones you value—washing the car, mowing the lawn, painting the lawn furniture, cooking on the barbecue, shopping for clothes or other items. A young child usually wants to do these important things too. When you allow your child into your sphere of activities, allow him enjoyable parts as well as the tedious ones. If he is washing the family car, allow the child to use the hose as well as to wash the wheels.

## The Cost of Inconvenience

Many consequences, particularly those for older children and adults, may at first seem trivial, but when put into practice their use may be extremely effective. For example, to have the father put a penny in a jar on the kitchen table every time he loses his temper may seem like a trivial act because he has plenty of pennies. But if the rule is strictly adhered to, the inconvenience of having to stop, get a penny, and go into the kitchen to put it in the jar can be extremely effective. It is not the cost as measured in terms of the money; it is the behavioral cost that is the effective aspect of this consequence.

As strategy for removing or reducing smoking behavior, many psychologists have employed the principle of inconvenience. For example, some heavy smokers have been instructed to keep exact records of their smoking behavior throughout each day. These people carry a notebook and pencil with them wherever they go and write down the time, to the minute, they take out a cigarette and light it and the amount of time that they spend smoking it. Some psychologists have also asked these people to collect the cigarette butts from their smoking and bring them in to be counted. Such tasks may not seem like direct consequences as they have been discussed throughout this book, but they are, in fact, consequences of a most annoying type. There comes a time when the smoker is just too busy to smoke if he must go through all the nonsense described above.

Another strategy of using inconvenience as a consequence was employed when a mother reported that her nineteen-year-old son continually disrupted the family by "checking things." On some evenings, he insisted on checking as many as seventy things before going to sleep. He checked to see if the back door was locked. He checked to see if the light was out in the basement. He checked to see if his pen was on his desk. He checked to see if his dresser drawers were closed. Obviously, some of these were reasonable checks and others were not. The situation became ludicrous, however, when he insisted on checking the same thing for the fifth time in the same evening.

At first his sleeping behavior was examined in relation to the possibility that the checking was an attention-getting behavior.

Some progress was made by reducing the parents' attention to the behavior and by providing conversation time before the boy went off to bed. The most effective thing, however, was to ask him to write down what he checked every time he checked it, what time he checked it, what the result of the check was, and what might have been the result if the item had been left unchecked. This procedure involved so much writing and decision making that it was nearly impossible for the boy to do seventy items each evening. As a matter of fact, the mere work, the inconvenience of the task, reduced the behavior to an acceptable frequency.

The same principles of inconvenience can work against the strategist in laying out his plan. For example, good homework behavior can be influenced by how convenient it is to get started. If there is a place designated, paper and pencil available, and a door that can be shut to prevent distraction, then the likelihood of the homework behavior's occurring consistently is greater than if there must be an annoyingly long time spent collecting materials and settling down to the job. This inconvenient routine can be a consequence that gains more control over the behavior than do consequences that occur after the performance.

## Check List for Consequences

We now turn to a number of questions that must be considered before the various consequences that you think of and discover through your observation and records can be used.

IS THE CONSEQUENCE A ONE-SHOT ERROR? / In the one-shot consequence, a parent uses a long-range threat as a consequence for a present behavior. Usually this threat involves the removal of an expected pleasant experience in the future, but the threat also may be stated in a positive manner, such as, "If you are a good boy, I might take you to the circus." Whichever way the one-shot consequence is used, it has the same disagreeable characteristics: it is not repeatable, and it seduces the parents into using threats, being unpleasant, and being arbitrary.

IS THE CONSEQUENCE TOO SEVERE? / Be sure that your selection of a consequence is not a reaction to one case of bad behavior. You want something that can be used repeatedly. As a matter of fact, the real test will come after things have settled down. The main feature of your plan that will help you through this test will be that you have planned to reward good behaviors as well as to punish bad ones. For this reason, you cannot make good plans when you are angry about your child's most recent error. When you are angry, you think only of his bad behavior and of ways to punish him. Cool off. Look at all sides. And remember that paying attention to bad behavior will not help. Select some consequence that can be used repeatedly and fairly. In addition, make sure your plan allows for rewards of the good behavior.

Withholding all allowance may be so severe a consequence that it is never used. In such cases, however, this severity may not limit you from ever using the consequence, but it may inhibit you from using it often enough to do any good. Because of this severe situation you will be trapped in the old habit of hoping and threatening but never doing anything but being quarrelsome.

IS THE CONSEQUENCE TOO WEAK? / What can be done if your child does not seem to care about the consequence? Possibly you are not really sticking to the rule and he really does not *have* to care. Possibly he has alternative free rewards ("If I can't watch TV, I'll go outside").

You may have decided that your daughter cannot have dessert until she has finished the food on her plate. But this will be ineffective if she is allowed a snack while watching TV. If she does not get dessert with dinner, she can get it later. Allowing alternative free rewards is no sin, but in this case it weakens the effectiveness of a rule. If you remove these alternative free rewards and find that after a few days your daughter still "just doesn't care," look carefully at the level of performance you require. Why can't she easily get this reward? Possibly you are asking for too much. Your demand may be reasonable, but it may be a great deal more than she was doing before. In this case, the step may be just too big. Your daughter was used to nibbling; now you fill her plate and tell her there will be no dessert until she finishes. Remember to start where she *is*, not where you *wish* her to be. Make sure you are "below her" in number and size of portions. The job cannot be done well and permanently in a single day.

Another possibility may be that she really doesn't care for desserts very much. If she doesn't, dessert is not a strong reward and other rewards are supporting the bad behavior. Consider the dinner situation once more. As we noted at the beginning of this chapter, the parents discuss all the events of their day, and conversation is punctuated with small aside remarks such as "Eat your peas," "Stop playing with your food," and "Finish up your milk or you won't get dessert." The only attention the child gets is for not eating. If more of the conversation were conducted in the child's areas of interest, she would have a chance to talk and also get some legitimate kinds of attention.

WILL THE SIBLINGS BE JEALOUS? / The most natural reasoning of siblings is: "We'll be bad so we can have goodies for getting better, too!" In some cases the reward may be something the siblings already have free; then there is no problem. But if it is some new incentive that they do not have, then, in fairness, the game will have to be open to them also. You may require a different behavior from them, however. They cannot be expected to stand by and not draw the conclusion stated above, but you can provide rewards for their good behaviors from the beginning.

WILL I FEEL HARD-HEARTED? / You won't have to feel hard-hearted if you plan to reward an existing level of behavior. If you plan to reward a behavior that you know will happen, you will not have to deprive your child but will merely use a better and more consistent set of rules. It will also help if you encourage effort and success verbally rather than make threats about the results of errors and failure.

## EXPERIMENT 11

### Testing the Rules

"Uncontrollable" boys[16] were assigned by the Juvenile Court to a special school. Five of the boys with "school behavior problems" were singled out for some special rules. Ranging in age from 11 to 15, they were a challenge for any teacher. One had assaulted a teacher as well as other students, two "talked back" and disrupted class, and two were always day-dreaming.

During a small summer class these boys were to work in a math workbook and follow some explicit rules written on the blackboard: do not leave seat without permission; do not talk without permission; do not look out the windows; do not tilt desks; do not make noise; do not disturb others.

Two half-hour classes were held under these rules each day. Observers counted rule violations and they also counted each complete ten-second interval in which studying continued throughout.

Each boy carried a report card home on which the teacher had marked the following categories: obeyed classroom rules; studied the whole period. For every day he received a "yes" in each category, he was awarded 1000 points to use to buy snacks, TV time, and permission to go outdoors. One "no" and all privileges were withheld for that day.

After observing 18 sessions without report cards (baseline), report cards were marked with "yes" for 20 sessions regardless of the behavior. After that, **real** consequences were used. A boy had to obey the rules 90% of the time, in order to get a "yes", in the "rule" category, and he had to study 90% of the time to get a "yes" in the study category. In Figures 4 and 5, this phase is indicated as "yes" and "no". "No back-up" means that during that phase privileges were free regardless of report card performance. Rules with a back-up really work!

HOW MANY RULES CAN I HAVE? / When you have the method by which to make very effective rules, it is tempting to construct a great many of them. But keep in mind that rules specifying a consequence take a great deal of time to carry out and require some responsibility on your part. There are so many things to

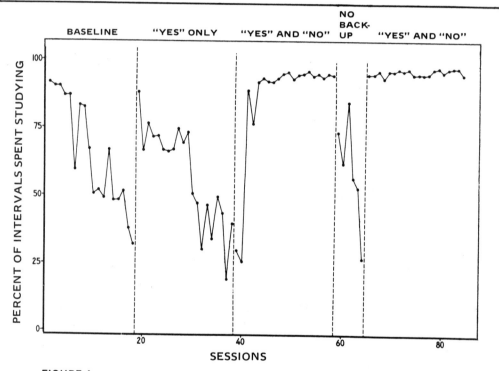

**FIGURE 4**

Percent of time intervals in which study behavior occurred.

(Adapted with permission of the **Journal of Applied Behavior Analysis.** Bailey, J.S., Wolf, M.M., and Phillips, E.L. "Home-based reinforcement and the modification of pre-delinquents' classroom behavior." **Journal of Applied Behavior Analysis.** 1970, 3, 227. Copyright 1971 by the Society for the Experimental Analysis of Behavior, Inc.)

change and there are so many things that you would like your children to learn that it is easy to fall into the trap of introducing too many rules at one time. When a child is bombarded with a great number of rules, he cannot make the usual discriminations as to what is good and what is bad. Further, the parent finds

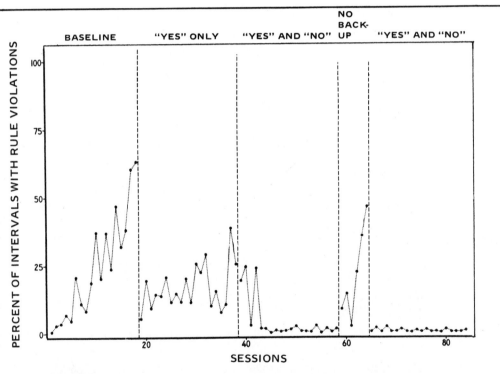

**FIGURE 5**
Percent of time intervals in which rule violations occurred.

(Adapted with permission of the **Journal of Applied Behavior Analysis.** Bailey, J.S., Wolf, M.M., and Phillips, E.L. "Home-based reinforcement and the modification of pre-delinquents' classroom behavior." **Journal of Applied Behavior Analysis.** 1970, 3, 227. Copyright 1971 by the Society for the Experimental Analysis of Behavior, Inc.)

himself giving out consequences for so many different things that
even he is confused. Everyone becomes so harassed and threatened that a great many errors occur on both sides. As the errors
pile up, the parent tends to punish these errors and to forget the
rules of positive reward, which have become too numerous to
handle.

If a child's parents are greatly concerned that she do just the
right things at the dinner table, they may establish enough rules
to ensure that she will do something wrong. *They* have come to
expect that she will do something wrong and are prepared to
reprimand her when she does it. *She* too has come to expect that
she will do something wrong and has expectations of the reprimand. With all these expectations, it is hard to have the additional
expectation of a pleasant dinner. So too many rules ensure that
errors will be frequent and that the family will have an unpleasant
time.

If parents can be patient enough to state only one rule in a
positive way so that successes can be rewarded, the child can
learn that rule successfully and, perhaps later, other ones. She can
gradually accumulate all those behaviors that are now being
demanded at once. Again, parents must dig back, ask for a small
part of what is wanted, reward that, and build from there.

HOW SHOULD THE RULE BE STATED? / Once you have established
a small and easily adhered to set of rules, you must learn to state
them as rules. When a rule involves a positive consequence, it is
tempting to prompt the child to perform so that you can give
him rewards. So you say, "Don't you want to eat nicely with
your spoon?" This is not a statement of the rule that praise will
occur when the spoon is used correctly. It is begging and
prompting by the parent, which is, in effect, attention for *not*
using the spoon. Learn to state the rules as a matter of fact: "As
long as you use the spoon, you can keep your ice cream."

Once you learn to inhibit the prompting and nagging behavior, the next pitfall is to let the child know in some nonverbal way that he is failing. For example, looking upset and glaring are common parental procedures that are supposed to tell the child he is wrong, but they also give the child attention for being wrong. If he is wrong, tell him so; use the rule as it was meant to be used or be quiet.

CAN SIBLINGS USE THE RULE? / Sometimes siblings want to play parent and use the rule on each other. For example, if you make the rule that a child can watch ten minutes of television for every one minute of practicing that he does on the piano, then you must face the question of what should be done when his sister says to him, "You'd better practice the piano or you won't get to watch television when I do." If you reprimand her for not minding her own business, you will probably strengthen her nosy behavior. You will also give indirect attention to her brother by protecting him when he has failed to practice.

Probably the most effective strategy is to make no comment at all when she gibes her brother. But the question that might come to your mind is why she can have all the television time she wants, particularly when she has the time and inclination to make such attempts to bother her brother. The rule here probably should be that the parent not interfere with the reactions and relationships between the children. This rule seems like good reasoning, because in most cases interference would be a kind of correction and coercion without any particular consequence to follow. An exception to this rule could be made for those circumstances in which the interference takes the form of a social encouragement—reward—for some good social behavior on the part of one of the children.

WILL THE RULE TAKE TOO MUCH TIME? / If you find that you have to constantly police your child to get a certain chore or behavior performed, you should reexamine the rule to find out how specific it is in its behavioral requirements. For example, if the rule is that the child must have his room cleaned up on Saturday morning before he can go out to play, you may find that you have to keep after him because "having his room cleaned up" has not been specifically defined and thus you and your child continually wrangle about whether or not the requirements have been met. One simple solution is to make up a check list of the things that must be accomplished before the room can be considered "cleaned up," and place the list on the bulletin board in the child's room. Items for such a check list might include "pillow in place, toys picked up, bedspread on straight." Even with such a list, of course, there will always be room for arguments if the child wants to find points to argue about. But the check list minimizes the opportunities for arguments and thus reduces the probabilities that they will occur.

WILL THERE BE TOO MUCH ARGUING? / Some rules are likely to elicit a great deal of pestering by the child in order to get you to break them or to get you to pay more attention to the fact that he isn't living up to them. In such a case, it might be well to write down the rule, not just in your own words, but in the words you intend to use when stating it to the child. If the rule is restated to the child every time the pestering begins, the situation is much clearer to him, he learns the rule faster, and the effect of your verbal attention is diminished because all you do is parrot the rule. You need not refrain from talking to him about other things, but when he asks about the rule you can avoid arguing with him about that.

If you find yourself using verbal embellishments of your rule rather than merely restating it, you might ask yourself, "Am I arguing about the rule because he believes I will break it and give in?" If you believe the child already understands the rule and the consequences specified, then there is no sense in continuing a long discussion of it. If he does not understand the rule, then a confusing set of verbal elaborations will not be helpful, whereas another restatement of the rule might be.

IS THE RULE TOO EXTREME? / At times adults are so frightened that things might get out of hand that they state extreme rules to make sure that bad behavior never gets started. It is common, for example, to find a teacher who allows absolutely no talking in her classroom—she is afraid that if she allows any talking in her classroom, things will get out of hand and an intolerable noise level will result. She has not been able to make up a rule that would result in a consequence for bad behavior yet allow the more acceptable levels of behavior. The rule becomes a problem because it prevents the practice of a tolerable level of behavior. In one case, this type of rule was in use in a special education class for the mentally retarded. Children who should have had as much experience trying to talk as could possibly be provided were working under a rule that prohibited all talking. The teacher was afraid that if the children started talking a little, they would talk too much. This is the ironic result of using extreme rules to avoid extreme behavior.

In a similar case, children were not allowed to speak at lunch lest the noise in the lunchroom reach an intolerable level. A rule was devised that allowed some talking without the danger of complete chaos. The rule was that the students at two tables out of the twenty in the lunchroom could talk each day. It turned out to be a very artificial rule, but at least it provided some latitude and some practice in social behaviors where before there had been none.

The usual rule used by the teachers in the lunchroom would never have been applied had the teachers in charge kept in mind the overall behavioral goal for the children. Of course, they wanted children very well versed in social and verbal behaviors and would not have done anything to divert progress from that goal. Once the goal was made explicit, it was obvious that the rule for the lunchroom would have to be changed. Thus, it is imperative to keep the overall behavioral goal in mind.

WHEN IS THE RULE IN EFFECT? / Are there circumstances under which the rule is not to be in effect? If so, these exceptions should be incorporated into the basic rule. If you do not intend to penalize a child for being noisy in the house when his father is not there, but you do intend to dock his allowance if he is noisy while his father is home, then the presence of the father should be stated in the rule. The child can more quickly learn the discrimination that you have, in effect, set up for him. Thus, if there is a discrimination involved, the best policy is to state it.

SHOULD THE CHILD BE FORCED? / At times your statement of the rule may imply that the child will be forced to comply with the rule if he does not do so voluntarily. When you say to a young child, "You must come home for dinner now," you imply that if he does not come home now, you will drag him home. If this is your intention, then that forcing of the behavior should be done immediately after a full statement of the rule has been given. Otherwise, you imply another rule: "You must come home for dinner or I will force you to come home for dinner, but you can delay it by haggling and putting me off for a while." If you adhere to this rule, then of course you must be prepared to do a great deal of haggling.

There are other rules, however, that cannot be followed by such coercion or by any other consequences that you might be willing to use, and therefore you should eliminate the use of such rules. These rules will have to be restated so that some positive consequence will follow. For example, "Eat your food" cannot ordinarily be followed by forcing the behavior if the child refuses. You could force the food down his throat, but it would be ridiculously unpleasant. Instead, you will have to provide some incentive to get the behaviors to occur and to get the rules to work. The implication must not be "Eat your food or I will force you," but rather "If you eat your food, then I will do something nice." If doing something nice for your child because he ate his food is an idea that you find unacceptable, then possibly the request that he eat his food should not have been made. If no reward (not even a social reward) is intended, then the behavior is literally too unimportant to bother with.

## OBJECTIVES *chapter four*

1. What is the goal of child rearing?

2. What is a good guideline for choosing consequences for children's behaviors?

3. Why does bad behavior often occur?

4. List two disadvantages of trying to arrange consequences for "nonbehaviors".

5. What is the danger of giving social reward at the wrong times?

6. What is the purpose of setting limits to consequences (e.g., a minimum allowance of 25 cents and a maximum of 75 cents)?

7. Give two examples of strategies using the principle of inconvenience.

8. Give an example of how inconvenience can work against planning.

9. What is a one-shot error?

10. Why isn't it a good idea to make plans when you are angry about your child's most recent error?

11. What are three reasons why a consequence might not have an effect?

12. How can the problem of sibling jealousy be handled?

13. What are two dangers of making too many rules?

14. What is the most effective strategy when siblings attempt to use the rule on each other?

15. What is an alternative to arguing with a child about a rule?

# 5 / *Spare the Rod*

For most parents punishment is a dangerous practice, because punishment is likely to be more related to the frustrations and moods of the parents than to the behaviors of the child. The result of frequent punishment is a child who attends the moods of his parents rather than his own rights and wrongs. The child becomes a manipulator. He knows that as long as he doesn't push too far he can misbehave and still avoid punishment by stopping at just the right time. An example is the child who shows off and acts silly when company comes. This child makes a fool of himself while watching his parents' embarrassment. He knows he can go a little further than usual because company is present and his parents don't want to be unpleasant. He can recognize the signs when *he* reaches *their* breaking point— and their breaking point is a better predictor of punishment than his own foolishness is. The child is thus paying more attention to his parents' mood than to his own actions.

Parents who give punishment on the basis of their feelings are continually agitated; they threaten punishment but are usually kept at a point of conflict by the child who is acting badly but not badly enough to be punished. Here again a strategy session must result in an explicitly stated *behavioral* definition that will signal consequences. Make sure that this definition is made in terms of the child's behavior—not in terms of your frustration and anger. It should not be applied when he pushes *you* too far but rather when *he* misbehaves in a given way. You might, for example, decide to scold your child and not serve his dessert whenever he spills his food at dinner. This scolding would provide a punishment as a result of the child's behavior, not as a result of your emotion. But before you use the rule, there are other effects to consider.

## The Crimes of Punishment

INCONSISTENCY / Consistency of experience is basic to learning. The lack of consistent rewards will only reduce the amount of encouragement and information the child gets. He will learn at a slower pace. But inconsistent punishment is quite another matter. It has a much greater effect than merely slowing down some learning. It may reduce other behaviors, even those you want to keep. Scolding a child at dinner now and then about spilled food may reduce the number of accidents, but it will also reduce his talking. Sometimes inconsistent punishment reduces *all* behavior, because the child can never be sure when punishment will come.

Because punishment is uncertain, he becomes very cautious, at least when he is around the person who punishes. When he is with other people, however, his bad behavior increases because the threat of punishment is there only when his mother is around, and the rest of the time he can let off steam. Problem behavior will continue as long as punishment is more related to the moods and frustrations of the parent than to actions of the child.

When punishments are very strictly related to the emotions of the parents, then there is consistency, of course. But here is another rule for the child to learn. The rule has changed. "If I do this, I get punished" can now be restated as "If I do this *when Mommy looks mad*, I get punished." This rule will result in the frustrating situation described above. In the long run, the child will learn to behave only when the punishing parent is around *and* angry. To control the child the parent then finds himself acting angry most of the time. The child may even learn to tell the difference between when the parent acts angry and when he really is angry, and the parent will be very agitated because only acting *really* angry will work. The parent has now been pushed up one more notch toward becoming a behavioral problem himself.

The child also learns that the punishment comes only from the parent and his anger. Baby-sitters and teachers will be fair game, and that will further limit the pleasantness of the parent's life.

DISCRIMINATION / We all develop discriminations and act differently with different people. But when punishment is involved, we do our best to avoid the punishing people altogether. The relationship that develops is one in which two persons are barely able to tolerate each other, one (the child) because of the possibility of being punished, the other (the parent) because of the uncomfortable behaviors that seem to be demanded by the situation.

On the other hand, consider the child who does *not* discriminate between the various emotions of his parents. A true lack of consistency may develop for a child who is too young to know when his mother is angry or when she is acting. Again, there really may be a consistency, but in this case the child cannot see it. The result may be that he ignores all punishments, because he cannot predict them. The punishments provide him with no information about how to change behavior in order to avoid punishment.

Almost everyone has known a child whose mother punished continually—for no (consistent) reason—while he continued to perform just as he pleased. To tolerate and resist punishment in this manner requires a certain kind of strength, and the child who uses this behavior is usually a rough-and-tumble boy. He comes into the house like a destructive storm. He seems to get some kind of delight out of angering his mother, and she provides much anger. He gives the impression that he feels challenged and that from his distorted point of view he is winning, in spite of the fact that he is always being punished.

Usually any suggestion by his mother of "something nice" to play is rejected, perhaps because it would mean that the game with her would be over. Other adults are suspicious about how much of his bad behavior has to do with her and may have said, "I'd like to have him under my control for a week or so, away from his mother. He'd shape up." The implication of that wish is

## EXPERIMENT 12

### Punishing Behavior: Limited Effects

Some very difficult children seem to require drastic action; for example those that are self-destructive. They bang their heads and arms against harmful objects, and bite or scratch themselves severely. Punishment — even electric shock — is justified when the mutilation caused by the behavior itself is much more severe than the shock or punishment. "Straight-jackets" for such "psychotic" or severely retarded children arrest many aspects of development but do nothing to reduce the problem, for whenever the children are released they begin again.

Linda and John were both eight-year-olds. Gregg[17] was eleven. When they came to the hospital it was necessary to keep them continuously bound, hand and foot, in order to see that they didn't damage themselves further. They all had multiple scars of the head and face, and became extremely agitated, kicking and beating on themselves when given the opportunity.

While such children are severely retarded it may be the case that these behaviors serve to attract attention. So, a physician and a psychologist began treating John by leaving him alone and unrestrained for daily morning sessions of one-and-a-half hours. Gregg was given the same treatment. Linda had damaged her ears so badly that such a risk couldn't be taken.

Observers counted self-destructive behaviors from behind a one-way mirror. They reported that John, without attention, decreased his rate of hitting, kicking, and biting from over 2,700 times per session to zero in 11 sessions. Gregg started out with a rate of about 800 but took much longer to get to zero.

However, in situations with people

that they would continue to use punishment but somehow use it more effectively—possibly more consistently. If that child is to get better someday, however, someone will have to (1) provide an opportunity for well-defined good behavior; (2) reward the good behavior heavily and consistently with a very desirable positive consequence; and (3) sharply limit the use of punishment to only the most obnoxious behaviors, and then use it very consistently without pleading or threatening. Obviously, planning and carrying out such steps are much harder tasks than the one some hard-headed uncle has in mind when he says he could "thrash it out of him." The job requires much more planning

present the destructive behaviors continued. So the experimenters used an electric shock delivered through a rod pressed to the child's leg. Only 12 such shocks completely eliminated the destructive behavior. As a result, the children exhibited many more affectionate and positive social responses. But these effects were selective and worked only where shock was given and only with those who had actually presented the shocks.

Mike[18] was a 14-year-old boy who was considered profoundly retarded. He didn't interact with others and stared or played with a speck of dirt when left alone. He would sometimes comply with requests such as "come here" but would not speak himself. But Mike bit other children severely, occasionally tore his clothes, destroyed furniture, decorations, toys, water faucets and electric sockets.

In an isolated setting where the behaviors could be accurately counted, a hand-held shocker was touched to Mike's forearm for these behaviors. In six 1½-hour sessions where bottles, pictures, and balloons were available for breaking, tearing, and popping, picture tearing stopped after three shocks. Thereafter, balloon breaking stopped with only one warning. Other temptations set before Mike were then easily controlled.

Beginning with at least ten incidents of destruction in each session, Mike showed no destructive behavior after these "shocking" experiences.

However, in a more realistic situation with other children the biting and destroying behaviors could not be controlled with warnings. Shock was again necessary before the problems decreased to nearly zero and Mike became sociable and co-operative.

than that. It requires strategy sessions to plan which good behaviors to work for, which rewards will be used for those good behaviors, and which obnoxious behaviors should still be punished rather than ignored.

WITHDRAWAL / Sometimes continual punishment creates a different kind of child than the one described above. Sometimes, the punishments are too much for a child to bear, too severe, too frequent; and the child's solution may be to stop responding altogether or, at least, to respond as little as possible. In this case inconsistent and frequent punishment has produced a very quiet and introverted child whose few tentative responses are likely to be pounced on with reprimands and corrections. Even when punishment is consistent and the child knows how to avoid it, why should he risk it in front of this dangerous person? The child will "withdraw" from this situation as far as he can. If he can *physically* withdraw to his room, the basement, or outside, he'll do that, too. The best description of a person who is being threatened with punishment is that he wants out. Only if escape from the situation is impossible will he try other solutions to avoid the punishment, such as changing his behavior.

Whenever punishment is used, then, the parent is counting on some other aspect of the situation to keep the subject within range of the punishment. Either the doors are locked, or the culture is backing the parents (children must live with their parents), or the other rewards are held by parents (room and board, and so on). No matter how effective and productive the punitive measures might be, the parent must look forward to the eventual loss of the child, unless other overwhelmingly positive events offset this effect.

Punishment situations become cues for the child to withdraw. For a child, the situation may be a schoolroom, a house, a time of day, a person, or a combination of these. The mere termination of punishment is not likely to be effective in encouraging the withdrawn child because he or she is unwilling to take chances and may never find out that punishment is not as likely to occur as it used to be. At some point the child refuses to try new behaviors or test the parent's reactions because it is too dangerous. The fear has become unreasonable, and the only solution the child is willing to accept is withdrawal.

In this case, a reduction in punishments *and* an increase in planned opportunities for rewards will help. When punishment has made the child timid, some very subtle things may act as punishments. Simply interrupting the child when he intends to say something at dinner may silence him for the whole meal. A verbal snap from his brother or sister may be enough to bring him to submission. He has become so vulnerable that he cannot be protected from the everyday encounters that have become punishments for him. It will require an isolated situation with the parent giving a great deal of planned social reward to draw him out. These isolated sessions will have a generalized effect if they are gradually held in more open places. For example, the parent might begin by playing a game or doing a puzzle with him each day in his room—alone. A great deal of encouragement and praise should be provided in these sessions, and they should be a daily habit. Arrangements should be made for the other children to be away at these times. It is dangerous even to have them sit and watch, because they will probably do more than that; they will provide the old verbal jabs that cause him so much trouble. Also, the jabs are cues that make him afraid, which is the last thing wanted now.

Once he is responding in this isolated session, the parent can begin to allow the others back in. The parent could even run some sessions in other parts of the house where he can respond well, in spite of others, because of the extra encouragement.

LOW FREQUENCY OF BEHAVIOR / The example above is an extreme case of the general effect of punishment, but even when used with consistency, punishment tends to reduce the overall output of behavior. In the punishment situation, a child becomes more careful about *all* his activities. He is less exploratory—a prospect that may bring great joy to some parents. Parents taking this road, however, must be careful to police their use of punishment so that it is determined by the child's behavior, not by their own frustrations. A low response rate is dangerous because the number of opportunities for reward is reduced because in general there is less behavior. Rewards cannot be given for behaviors that never happen.

This low rate of behavior becomes very specific to the people who punish. That is, it may occur only in the presence of the punishing person, because he presents the threat. So with any punishment a kind of conditioning can take place: the presence of the punisher is a signal for no behavior, and therefore his opportunities to exert an influence on anything are reduced. When this point is reached, a parent doesn't have to punish the teen-ager to get him to stop talking. All he has to do is enter the room. Why? The teen-ager could explain, "Because he always bugs me [reprimands, lays down more rules for me, punishes me] every time I do anything or tell him anything." The very presence of a person who is likely to criticize or punish is enough to stop everything.

In one case, the parents of a teen-ager who was in police custody for vandalism were interviewed to find out how much responsibility they took in rearing their daughter. The mother stated that she could not guess where her daughter was when she was arrested. When asked where her daughter usually went on her nights out, she answered, "Oh, I don't know. She never talks to me." "When was the last time she told you about school or activities with friends?" she was asked. "I can't even remember," she said. "Oh, yes, now I remember, she told me what one of those bad boys said about her figure—just as if she were proud of having boys think of her that way!" When asked what her reaction was, the mother answered with some pride, "*Well*, I told her that if I *ever* saw her with that boy again, I'd give her the whipping of her life!"

What do you suppose the daughter learned from this little exchange with her mother? To leave some boys alone and not talk to them? Or to leave her mother alone and not talk to her?

LOW FREQUENCY OF REWARD / When punishment is the most frequent consequence, it is hard to use rewards also. First, the parents are busy giving punishments for bad behaviors rather than looking for good behaviors to reward. Second, the good behaviors that the parents could be looking for occur less often as a side effect of the frequent punishment. This type of reticence happens only in the presence of the parents, because they are the ones who create the situation. Elsewhere—with peers, for example—the child may be much more active, which is one reason that peers have more opportunity to reward and influence a child than parents do. When that happens, parents are replaced as the primary source of rewards, and then, of course, as the primary influence. Friendliness and good relationships really amount to this: Some people try and are successful at finding things to reward; therefore, they see a lot more behavior and are more likely to be influential. Other people try and are successful at finding things to punish; such people see fewer behaviors and therefore have less opportunity to influence those behaviors.

THE ONE-SHOT PUNISHMENT / The behavioristic approach taken in this book has as its most basic rule the repetition of consequences. And, as was noted previously, the one shot is the unrepeatable, often-threatened consequence.

When the punishment involved is a one shot, a parent is tempted to threaten and nag a great deal. Usually a one-shot punishment is a strong punishment, and the parent wants to get as much out of it as he can. He really doesn't want to use the punishment; he hopes to bluff his way through.

When a parent bluffs and uses such infrequent or even nonexistent punishments, the child quickly learns the system and plays a game in brinkmanship. From calling earlier bluffs the child has learned how best to use the situation—and he is now in control of it. Moreover, the bluff not only creates a climate of threats and nagging but also may attract a kind of attention from the parent that works as a reward for bad behavior rather than as a punishment.

---

## EXPERIMENT 13

### Programmed Punishment

Miss C[19] was a compulsive eater weighing in at 181 pounds. In three weeks of observation before treatment (baseline) she ate 200 pieces of candy a week, cookies and doughnuts by the dozens, and pizza and ice cream one to three times each day. One thing she **didn't** like (there seemed to be very few) was smoking. When she tried it, she became nauseous and dizzy.

Miss C was asked to light a cigarette, take a bite of her favorite food (candy), chew it, but before swallowing, she was to take one long "drag" on the cigarette and spit out the food saying, "Eating this junk makes me sick", which it did. She was asked to repeat this procedure ten times twice a day using different types of candy.

By the 11th week candy consumption had dropped to zero and cookies were attacked next, then doughnuts in Week 15. Her weight at Week 11 was down to 166,

by Week 15 it was down to 155, by Week 18 to 140, by Week 21 to 132, and by Week 24 to 128. Figure 6 shows the progress in controlling eating. No, Miss C. never took up smoking!

Twenty-five slouching adults[20] volunteered to wear a harness that sounded a warning click whenever slouching occurred and, if not corrected, the click was followed three seconds later by a loud embarrassing tone from the apparatus under their clothes. The apparatus also measured time spent slouching.

Every hour or two the loud tone was turned on or off so that "baseline" (without the consequence) could be compared with "conditioning" (with the consequence).

The embarrassing noise (social punishment) was enough to reduce slouching time 90% or more for half of the subjects. The other half reduced slouching time over 62%.

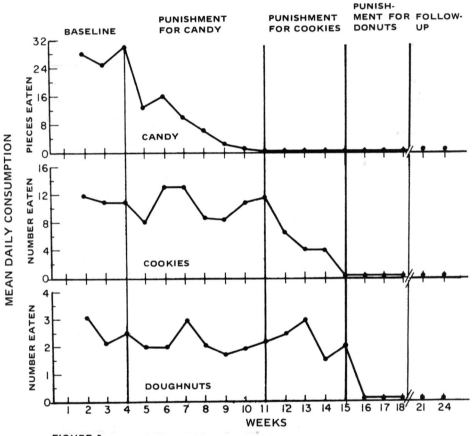

**FIGURE 6**
Mean daily consumption of candy, cookies, and doughnuts as a function of punishment.

(Adapted with permission of **Behavior Therapy.** Morganstern, K.P., "Cigarette smoke as a noxious stimulus in self-managed aversion therapy for compulsive eating: Technique and case illustration." **Behavior Therapy.** 1974, 5, 257.

## Parental Penal Codes

The use of punishment creates so many discouraging problems that parents might be expected to stop using it, but there are several reasons why it continues to be so common. First, punishment has an immediate effect. It usually breaks up an ongoing flow of bad behavior and temporarily stops the misbehaving. It is also a tension releaser for the parent, so that teaching the child a lesson disguises the real reason, which is evening the score. Finally, under some conditions punishment is effective in a lasting way. To select effective uses of punishment, however, some types of punishment and rules for using them must be considered.

There are several kinds of rules for the use of punishment. In most cases these rules state the conditions under which a painful or aversive event will occur. The rule may allow the child to predict that he will be punished on the basis of some warning. For example, the child may be able to look at his mother's face and get a warning about whether punishment will follow bad behavior. He may also know situations in which he will be punished if he does not respond correctly. He may have learned, for example, that if he does not do his homework before his father comes home, his father will punish him. There are many other kinds of rules concerned with punishment, and they must be sorted out so that their advantages and disadvantages can be specified.

THE TRUE PUNISHMENT RULE / The first and most common rule concerns true punishment. This rule states that a certain bad behavior will be followed by something painful, aversive, or unwanted. The purpose of the rule is to reduce the frequency of a behavior. If a teacher does not want students to be away from their desks, she might state a true punishment rule: "If a student gets up from his desk, he will be sent to the principal's office." At home, the following might be a true punishment rule: "If a child pulls his sister's hair, he will be spanked." Such a rule can be very effective if it is followed consistently.

Sometimes a warning is given after a true punishment rule has been stated. A mother might say, "Don't pull your sister's hair or I'll spank you." The warning may be, as in this case, a mere restating of the rule, or it may be the actual process of getting out the switch or belt. One problem that occurs when a warning is given is that this warning may become a consequence for the bad behavior instead of a warning. If, for example, the true punishment rule has been stated as "When books are pulled out of the bookcase, punishment will be given," but when they are pulled down the mother says, "If you do that *again* I am going to punish you," the warning is a consequence, because *it* occurs after the bad behavior. We cannot be sure what this new kind of consequence is. Perhaps it provides information about a more painful punishment that will follow the behavior the next time it occurs. Perhaps it is attention that is really a reward for bad behavior. So the simple rule of true punishment can become complicated when a warning is added. Because of this complication, it is best to label the warning situation as something special. The label usually given to this situation is "classical avoidance."

THE CLASSICAL AVOIDANCE RULE / The classical avoidance rule states that if a certain warning (or situation) *does* occur and a behavior *does not* occur, then the child will be punished. The child must learn a signal that will help him avoid the punishment. Thus, you might say, "Be nice to your sister and do not pull her hair, or I will punish you." Now the warning has been given with the rule; if the child does not act in a certain (nice) way, he is supposed to be punished. The difficulty with the classical avoidance rule is that it specifies a particular situation in which the behavior will be punished, namely, when there is a warning.

Many loving parents find themselves trapped by this rule, because they always feel that the child deserves a warning. Once the child learns that he deserves a warning, he knows that he is completely safe and can be as bad as he likes until he hears the warning. In other words, the rule is designed to control only a minute part of behavior, and although it does that very well, no general change in the child can be expected. For example, a grade-school teacher may call the principal to the classroom because a student is being particularly bad. The rule in effect is that if the principal comes to the classroom *and* the student *does not* stop misbehaving, then some drastic action will be taken. This drastic action or punishment usually takes the form of the removal of some privilege or possibly the calling of the parents. On

## EXPERIMENT 14

### A First Alternative to Punishment: Ignoring and Praising

Clif and Frank[21] were in Mrs. A's second grade class. Clif spent almost all of his time playing with objects in or on his desk. He frequently bothered others around him. He wrote on his shoes or arms and threw kisses to the girls. The other children had stopped paying attention to him so all this behavior looked rather lonely. A sign he made for his desk said, "Do You Love Me?".

Frank's behavior was also a problem. He fought at recess, and like Clif, he often disrupted class by running around, talking, and bothering others. Reprimanding and discipline had no effect.

In Mrs. B's class was a third child, Stan, who was very wild. He ran from place to place grabbing and biting others, stealing when he could, and swearing pro-

fusely.

Observers began counting the boys' behaviors. Inappropriate behaviors were: getting out of seat, running, making noise with objects or feet, grabbing other people's belongings, biting, fighting, talking when asked not to, whistling, screaming, ignoring the teacher, chewing on objects, etc. (There were lots of things to correct!) Appropriate behaviors were: working as assigned for ten seconds.

After some baseline observation, the teachers were asked to make some very exact rules to be placed on their classroom bulletin boards such as, "don't talk to your neighbors" or "sit quietly while working". Teachers repeated the rules about five times a day out loud.

In the next phase of the experiment a few weeks later, Mrs. A and Mrs. B were asked to ignore all of these inappropriate behaviors. Instead of saying, "Clif, you the other hand, if the student stops acting up, then the drastic action is not taken. The student can be brought under control very easily because he has learned a discrimination, but, as every teacher knows, the response to the principal becomes increasingly limited to his presence. When the principal is not there, the student tends to misbehave just as much as ever.

SUPPRESSION / A special case of the classical avoidance rule is called suppression. It is the same rule as classical avoidance but without the usual escape clause. In this case the rule states that if a

know you are supposed to be working"; or "Frank, will you stop bothering your neighbors"; or "Stan, you have been at the window a long time"; "Clif, sit down!"; "Frank, stop rocking your . . .", etc.; the teachers were asked to say nothing. They were to ignore all instances of bad behavior of all students in the classes except when they thought someone was about to be hurt.

After some weeks, praise was added. Mrs. A and Mrs. B were to "catch the children being good", give praise, a smile, or attention instead of letting the good behavior go largely unnoticed as was common. This helped Mrs. A and Mrs. B with ignoring inappropriate behavior because they could now turn their attention to some other child saying, "I like the way you're working, Clif", or, "That's a very good job, Stan", or, "You're doing fine, Frank."

The graphs in Figures 7 and 8 show that improvement was best under this last condition. Mrs. A said, "I was amazed at the difference . . . [and] became convinced that a positive approach to discipline was the answer." Mrs. B even began training her classroom aide to ignore bad behavior.

**Other Changes:** Clif's behavior got worse in the "ignore phase" and didn't improve until praise was added. Mrs. A had difficulty finding something praiseworthy about him but when she did, his behavior changed rapidly. Frank also required that praise for improvement. Mrs. B reported that, "Stan has changed from a sullen, morose, muttering, angry individual into a boy whose smile seems to cover his whole face."

The teachers were beginning to enjoy their classes!

certain warning (or situation) occurs, then the child will be
punished regardless of how his behavior changes after the warning. This warning has no deal built in. There is no way to avoid
the punishment—the child is merely told to prepare for the
inescapable consequence. In the school example the rule would be
that if the principal enters the classroom, he *will* call the student's
mother. In this case the student's poor behavior may be sup-
pressed when the principal arrives. But if the rule is followed, the
student's mother will be called whenever the principal goes to the
classroom, regardless of whether or not the student behaves well.

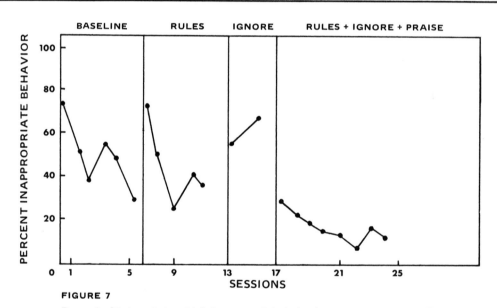

**FIGURE 7**

Percent of intervals in which inappropriate behavior occurred under different
rule conditions for Clif.

(Adapted with permission of the **Journal of Applied Behavior Analysis.** Madsen,
C.H., Becker, W.C., Thomas, D.R. "Rules, praise and ignoring: Elements of ele-
mentary classroom control." **Journal of Applied Behavior Analysis.** 1968, 1, 146.
Copyright 1968 by the Society for the Experimental Analysis of Behavior, Inc.)

Why does the child usually change his behavior as a result of the warning, even though the punishment is inevitable? Such a change in behavior seems unreasonable. The reason may be that there really is some escape clause in the rule, though it was not stated as an escape clause. The more bad behavior the student shows after the warning, the worse the inevitable punishment might be. In this case the presence of the principal is, in itself, a punishment, because it indicates that punishment is inevitable. But again, the behavior controlled by such a rule is specific to a person or a situation.

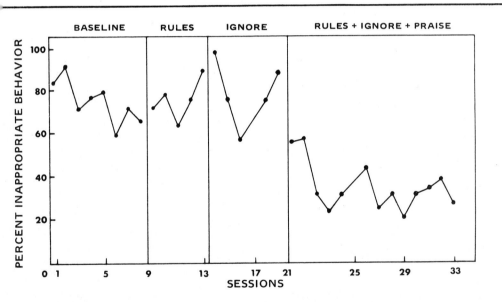

**FIGURE 8**
Percent of intervals in which inappropriate behavior occurred under different rule conditions for Stan.

(Adapted with permission of the **Journal of Applied Behavior Analysis.** Madsen, C.H., Becker, W.C., Thomas, D.R. "Rules, praise and ignoring: Elements of elementary classroom control." **Journal of Applied Behavior Analysis.** 1968, 1, 147. Copyright 1968 by the Society for the Experimental Analysis of Behavior, Inc.)

A "POSITIVE" APPROACH / One common avoidance procedure takes a slightly more positive approach to the rules about punishment and states what behavior is demanded to avoid punishment rather than what behavior or situation will produce punishment. A common school example here is the rule that if the student completes two pages of his workbook, then he will not have to remain after school. At least this rule has the advantage of telling the child what we want him to do instead of merely suggesting what the bad behaviors are. The rule still does not explain why the child would like to be under the rule, but it does have its

---

# EXPERIMENT 15

## A Second Alternative to Punishment: Time Out

Remember Rorey B. in Experiment 2? His mother placed him in his room for a short time when he was misbehaving. This procedure is sometimes called **time out** because hopefully it's time out from any opportunity for reward — social or otherwise.

Technically, time out is an event which can decrease the behavior it follows and, therefore, is a kind of **punishment**. But it's not usually referred to as such. It doesn't follow the old notion of punishment: inflicting pain and suffering. Ignoring might be called time out. But when an adult ignores a child's bad behavior other people may still provide attention. Time out, for that reason, usually means that a little more effort goes into seeing that no opportunity for reward is

possible (such as sending the child to an isolated room where there is very little reward or play-opportunity available).

Due to brain damage, five-year-old Ray[22] didn't talk or take verbal directions. However, he had learned to imitate his teacher in his speech training center through the use of praise (i.e., "good"), and ice cream, as consequences for good performance. But Ray began a bad habit of making all kinds of inappropriate vocal noises. The teacher had to wait, ignore the nonsense, and when Ray had finished fooling around, present the next sound he was to practice imitating. Although the jabbering went unrewarded, it continued.

Time out was used as a consequence for Ray's jabbering. The teacher picked up the ice cream and turned her back to him until he stopped. The time out procedure involved ignoring that behavior, socially "cutting him off" by turning away, and positive side; it states what we would like him to do. Of course, even under this rule the child would still rather be someplace where there is no threat of punishment at all. In spite of some positive advantages, this avoidance procedure produces a minimum level of performance. The child only wants to produce the amount of good behavior necessary to avoid the punishment. When under such a threatening situation, a child would not want to produce any more good behavior than necessary. So you can never expect a child to blossom out or to continue on his own when he has learned to perform under such a threat. It can be a

removing any other available rewards, such as the ice cream.

Four time outs were used at the end of a training session where jabbering was occurring at least two times per minute. The rate of jabbering dropped to zero and remained there while appropriate speech increased. Entire 20-minute periods went by with no verbal nonsense.

Tom[23] (age nine) experienced a different kind of time out for his disruptive classroom behavior. He had already frustrated his parents and the teacher, who had tried taking away recess time and gym time, keeping him after school, sending him to the principal, and using tranquilizing drugs (on the child, that is), in order to control disruptive behavior.

A small gray, wooden booth was placed in the hall outside the classroom. It had a chair and table. Although it had no top, the booth was five feet high so Tom couldn't see out. Anytime an observer saw him out of his seat or talking without permission, the observer turned on a little red light which had been placed on Tom's desk. He had been told that every time he left his seat, or talked, the light would go on. Further, each time it went on he would lose five minutes of gym or recess, which would have to be spent in the booth.

Prior to this time-out procedure, the observer had counted Tom's bad behaviors both under the usual circumstances (baseline), and when the teacher instructed Tom to sit down and keep quiet. Then the observer counted the bad behaviors during time out and after it was discontinued (contingencies removed). The results are in Figure 9.

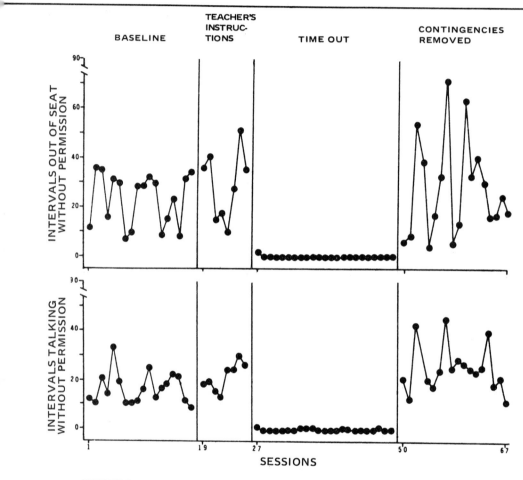

**FIGURE 9**

Intervals of talking or being out of seat for the subject during daily sessions.

(Adapted with permission of the **Journal of Applied Behavior Analysis.** Ramp, E., Ulrich, R., and Dulaney, S. "Delayed time out as a procedure for reducing disruptive classroom behavior: A case study." **Journal of Applied Behavior Analysis.** 1971, 4, 237. Copyright 1971 by the Society for the Experimental Analysis of Behavior, Inc.)

useful and effective device for producing a particular good behavior in a particular circumstance, but you cannot produce any
lasting effects in situations where the threat is not present.

Avoidance procedures such as those described above are just
as commonly used by children as they are by parents. For example, a teen-ager may do a lot of grumbling (a kind of punishment) if his parents ask for "too much." If he is asked to clean up
his room before he goes to school in the morning, then he starts
to complain. In this case the parent is under a kind of avoidance
control. If she makes his bed and refrains from asking him to do
it, she will not be punished. One could also state this sequence as a
true punishment rule: If she asks him, he punishes her. At times,
screaming and other kinds of bad deportment are used by children in a similar way.

Common reactions of the parents to this situation are (1) to
give in and do what the children demand, (2) to do their work
for them to avoid the hassle, or (3) to punish *them* for trying to
punish. The last alternative leads to a real trading of blows, for
competition has developed that perpetuates itself. Who will be
mature enough to recognize this folly for what it is and stop
punishing?

Someone will have to make up some new rules, someone
whose experience and thoughtfulness allow him to see that the
punishing contest will not contribute to long-range goals. In
other words, someone will have to have enough love to start
looking for something to reward rather than for something to
punish, and it is the parents who must take this fresh start. If they
do not, there is little chance that their child will.

## Eliminating Consequences

REMOVING REWARD / Removing a reward usually reduces the
frequency of a behavior. At first, there may be an increase in bad
behavior (for example, if attention is no longer given for tantrums). But if the rule is maintained, the behavior weakens in a

process called *extinction*. Extinction is a change in behavior due to practice (practice with the consequence removed), and the principle of consistency applies here too. As a matter of fact, inconsistency in extinction may create more problems than existed previously. Suppose that you usually go into your house through a side door, but one day when you turn the knob, the door will not open. Your initial reaction may be to calmly try the key, but if the door still does not open, you may resort to giving it a kick before giving up and going around to the front door. If, however, high humidity has made the door stick and a kick in fact opens it, you may very readily learn this new behavior and "superstitiously" kick the door each time you enter. On the other hand, if the kicks were effective only in giving you a sore toe, this behavior would quickly extinguish and you would seek an effective, consistent method of getting the door open.

If an extinction procedure is to work, the rule must be maintained, so that a child learns, for example, that increasing or prolonging tantrum behavior will fail to bring a payoff. As a matter of fact, if the parents tried to extinguish crying by ignoring the child and his demands but gave in when it became too loud, too long, or too intense, they essentially withheld their reward until the behavior reached the level they were "demanding." Now the loud, long, intense crying is called a tantrum. Many prolonged emotional behaviors of children are a result of such on-again–off-again extinction procedures. If a little reward is added to that arrangement (such as providing whatever was being demanded by the tantrum), an effective means of developing bad behavior has been constructed.

Extinction, then, must be continued with great consistency to be effective in changing behavior. But while you are being steadfast in applying the extinction rule, do not repeat it too often or follow the example of a mother who was trying to extinguish her child's tantrum in a store by yelling (in order to be heard over his crying), "I'm not going to give in. You're not getting anything from me for that!" Of course, he *was* getting plenty from her for that. The rule should be stated clearly and firmly, and it should be repeated in the same words each time. No attempt should be made, however, to use the statement of the rule as a punishment. It is merely meant to be information, not attention or punishment. Extinction should be the lack of *any* consequence.

REMOVING PUNISHMENT / Stopping the use of punishment and avoidance procedures has another special problem. Many times the event that has been trained is the *lack* of something—the avoidance of a punishment or the inhibition of a behavior. Suppose that a girl has been badly frightened by a vicious dog. She has, we could say, been punished for being near a dog, and this punishment was so strong that the child now fears being near all dogs. If she approaches another dog, it will probably be friendly—most dogs are friendly, not vicious—so the threat of the punishment is really gone. Extinction has begun. But the child doesn't know this, and she continues her avoidance behavior, never testing to see if it is still a reasonable reaction. She could be on extinction for years and never know it. The fact that punishment is unlikely makes no change in her behavior. If only a slight inconsistency is added (an unfriendly dog every two or three years), the behavior is likely to continue forever.

As another example of the difficulties involved in the extinction of avoidance behavior, consider the dilemma of parents who scold their children about small misbehaviors in an effort to avoid bigger problems. These parents believe the old adage "Give 'em an inch, and they'll take a mile." The type of rules they apply may include "No running in the house," "No getting up from the table during dinner," and "No taking sand out of the sandbox." The parents probably won't stop using such rules to see if they are still necessary. They may never try giving the inch to see if the child would still try to take the mile. A rule may become unnecessary, and it may be an unrealistic limitation on the child as he grows up. The parents believe that if they do not reprimand small bad behaviors, they will be punished by the child, who will misbehave in worse ways. They are reluctant to stop reprimanding and see if they will still be punished. The parents may never give the situation a fair test, just as the child who is afraid of dogs never gives new dogs a fair test. Both continue to act out slightly miserable situations in order to avoid what they think would be very miserable ones. Yet extinction may have begun years ago. The child has grown and may not need a troublesome rule to control him. Thus, the problem with using avoidance extinction is that the child may never respond in a way that will enable the parents to find out that extinction has begun. And the information that extinction has begun is crucial to a change in behavior.

In many cases even when a reward has been in effect the change to extinction may not be apparent, particularly if the

## EXPERIMENT 16

### A Third Alternative to Punishment: Response Cost

Larry[24] had trouble going to sleep at night. Although he was 17 years old, he still insisted on coming to his mother at bedtime to talk about all of his worries. These visits often extended to three hours. Sleeping drugs, psychoanalysis, and tranquilizers had been ineffective over a six-month period.

Two strategies were used simultaneously. First, Larry was told that he would have a special time early in the evening to talk about his worries. If he came to his mother later, after bedtime, the next evening's special time would be cancelled. Second, the experimenter asked Larry to record many things about his problem: the time he went to his room for sleep, approximate time he remembered falling asleep, things he worried about, whether or not he used sleeping pills each night, etc. His mother recorded how often and when he came to talk about his worries.

The procedure was very burdensome for Larry. It discouraged him from worrying and complaining because he had promised to write all of it down. It "cost" too much effort to worry at night. It was too inconvenient, and, in addition, he lost his early evening session with his

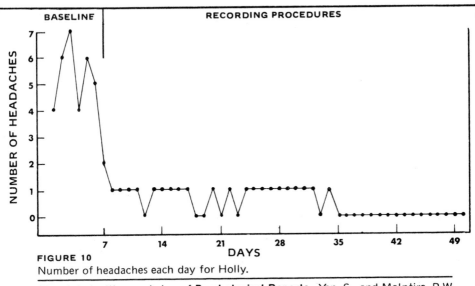

**FIGURE 10**
Number of headaches each day for Holly.

(Reprinted with permission of **Psychological Reports.** Yen, S., and McIntire, R.W. "Operant therapy for constant headache complaints: A simple response-cost approach." **Psychological Reports.** 1971, 28, 269.

mother for the next night. The number of nights in which he disturbed his mother at least once after bedtime dropped from seven nights a week to zero within three weeks. The time in which he went to sleep went from an average of three hours to 25 minutes.

He used the earlier time his mother offered to discuss his problems.

Holly[25] was 14 and complained of headaches at very suspicious times (just before school, when chores were to be done, etc.). Sometimes these complaints occurred as often as seven times a day. Her physician found nothing wrong. Like Larry, Holly was asked to record a number of things about the behavior: probable cause of headache, what would happen if she didn't have it when she had it, how long it lasted, what she did about it, etc. The procedure was a bigger hassle than the headaches and as a result the headaches decreased in frequency to zero. (See Figure 10)

These are response-cost procedures. They make the behavior "cost" more, in terms of energy or inconvenience, and thus the procedure tips the balance of benefit and cost. Later experiments will show this same cost procedure applied to money, allowances, and merit points.

behavior has not been followed by a consequence every time, anyway. Going from occasional reward to complete extinction (as in the example of the stuck door) may not be at all obvious. Under such conditions it may be more effective to draw the child's attention to the behavior before beginning extinction; to

---

## EXPERIMENT 17

### A Fourth Alternative to Punishment: Overcorrection

Logical consequences may not always be the common consequences. It may be difficult to arrange the situation so that the subject "suffers the consequences" of his bad behavior. But when it's possible to arrange logical consequences they are very effective.

Barbara (eight years old) and Wilma[26] (seven) had very low intelligence scores and attended a special day-care center. Both had an annoying habit which interfered with learning — they mouthed. Barbara put all kinds of objects in her mouth, or licked them or sucked them and, if the object was too big to lift, she went to it. Wilma just worked on her own hands. Possibly, the girls did these things for the attention they attracted, or because they received so little attention in general.

The experimenters considered using physical punishment to eliminate "mouthing". They also decided to try putting some bitter-tasting solution on Wilma's hands. They tested their procedures in a small room where the girls were to learn

the names of toys. Observers (and the parents) counted the mouthing behaviors in one-minute intervals. Sometimes rewards were given freely by the teacher on cue from a timer — independent of the child's behavior (called "noncontingent reinforcement", presented in Figure 11). Sometimes, the experimenters gave rewards (candy or sugar-coated cereal) to the child when she was not mouthing. On other occasions the child was slapped on the thigh for mouthing or the child's hands were painted with the bitter solution.

Overcorrection was an additional procedure. Whenever mouthing occurred the girl was told "no", and her teeth and gums were brushed with a toothbrush soaked in an oral antiseptic. Then the girl was dried off with a washcloth and learning continued. This procedure is called overcorrection because it presents the logical correction (an unclean object presents germs, therefore cleaning the mouth is logical), but it is overdone to provide a real deterrent to the bad behavior. You can see from the graph in Figure 11 that this procedure worked the best.

Could overcorrection be used for

overplay it to the point of embarrassment might be good preparation for extinction. This method may be usable in the case of the tantrum or in the case of disruptive classroom behavior.

## Punishment as a Reward

In the light of our discussion of tantrums, it should not be

other "compulsive" behaviors? Could the procedure work on a larger scale in a more realistic environment? The experimenters decided to try it on other behaviors in a more normal classroom using two new subjects.

Tricia and Mike were attending the same day-center as Barbara and Wilma. Their problems were compulsive head-turning (Tricia), and hand-clapping (Mike). These children were added to the experimental group and baseline data were recorded, but now the large playroom was used and the procedure carried out for the entire six-hour period each day. After baseline, overcorrection was applied in this new situation for 20 days, then baseline (no controlled consequences) for three more days. Then 12 more days of overcorrection were added. And last, a verbal warning, "stop that", was used alone for the first bad behavior of the morning and the first of the afternoon; all other occurrences were followed with overcorrection. The last phase consisted of providing Tricia and Mike with only a warning for their mistakes.

Tricia's overcorrection procedure consisted of asking her to put her head up, down, right, left when told to do so (instead of bobbing in an uncontrolled, unrequested way). This is easy and far less inconvenient than having your teeth brushed. So the time spent overcorrecting Tricia was extended from two to 20 minutes. With this time-consuming exercise as a consequence, Tricia's head-weaving dropped to zero.

Mike's hand-clapping went quickly to zero when "drilled" on hand positions for disruptive clapping. He was told, "Put your hands above your head, Mike", and "Put your hands in pockets, Mike", etc. If he didn't obey her, the teacher did it for him as she did for Tricia when she failed to put her head up or down, left or right. Each position was to be held for 15 seconds.

While such procedures may seem strict, they were not excessive. Within only a few days the behavior approached zero and overcorrection was required very infrequently. And, later, a verbal warning was usually enough. Now learning could progress for children who needed learning so very much.

surprising that some aversive actions on the part of the parents are rewards although they are intended to be punishments. This situation is most quickly exposed when parents complain that their child is continually testing them. Every time the parents lay down or threaten to establish a new rule that has a punishment as

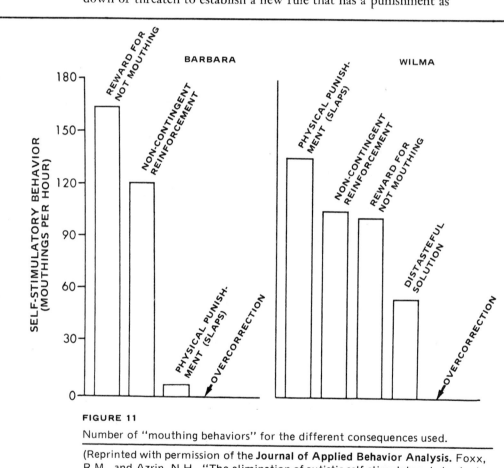

**FIGURE 11**

Number of "mouthing behaviors" for the different consequences used.

(Reprinted with permission of the **Journal of Applied Behavior Analysis.** Foxx, R.M., and Azrin, N.H. "The elimination of autistic self-stimulatory behavior by overcorrection." **Journal of Applied Behavior Analysis.** 1973, 6, 5. Copyright 1973 by the Society for the Experimental Analysis of Behavior, Inc.)

its consequence, the child cannot wait to try it out. There are at least two factors working here. The first is the adventure of taking a chance. The chase itself may be fun for the child, even if he is caught every time. Second, some uncontrolled aspect of the punishment itself may be rewarding. For example, a child who was punished by being forced to sit on a bench in front of the principal's office was having a great time being giggled at as he made attempts to hit and trip other students passing back and forth between classrooms. The child was described as a nuisance who did not care if he was punished. He cared. That's why he was a nuisance.

## OBJECTIVES  *chapter five*

1.  What are some effects of inconsistent punishment?

2.  What are some of the effects of punishment that must be considered before its use?

3.  Why is a low rate of behavior dangerous?

4.  Why does the frequent use of punishment make it hard to use rewards too?

5.  What is a "one-shot punishment", and what are its disadvantages?

6.  If punishment has so many undesirable side effects, why do people still continue to use it?

7.  In most cases, what does a punishment rule state?

8.  What is the rule of true punishment? What is its purpose?

9.  How may a warning become a consequence for bad behavior rather than a warning?

10. What is the classical avoidance rule? What is the problem with this rule?

11. What is the special case of the classical avoidance rule which is called the suppression rule?

12. How does the positive approach differ from the other punishment rules?

13. Give an example of the positive approach.

14. Give an example of how avoidance procedures can be used by children as they are by parents.

15. What are the three common reactions of parents to being punished by the child?

16. Define extinction.

17. What may be the child's first reaction to the removal of a reward?

18. What is the long-term effect of extinction?

19. Explain how "tantrum behavior" can be the result of inconsistent extinction.

20. What are two difficulties with the extinction of avoidance behavior?

# 6 / Means and Ends

A little girl may be more successful in her first attempts at cooking if all the ingredients and utensils are on a kitchen table rather than on a high counter or in a cabinet that she can't reach. She may learn to mow the lawn neatly if she is first assigned a small and uncomplicated portion of the yard. Thus, while controlling and changing the behavior of children, parents can be helpful by planning the conditions of practice as well as by planning the consequences. The practice of a behavior can be carried out in a situation that will cause the child to make many mistakes or in a situation that will increase his chances of performing successfully.

The first steps in learning behaviors are so crucial that they deserve special attention to see that the situations in which they are taken are as favorable as possible. And you *can* design the opportunities for practice so that errors are impossible or, at least, so that successes—and rewards—are probable.

## An Ounce of Prevention

Sometimes it is not necessary to use consequences to control behavior. As a parent, you can use restrictions on your child's practice to ensure that no mistakes will occur. Designing practice in this way can be a very simple process. It is easy to construct some situations so that a certain bad behavior is impossible. Not keeping a cookie jar might be easier than trying to teach your child not to steal from it. Buying a lock for the medicine cabinet might be better than trying to teach a four-year-old to respect medicines. Sending fighting children to separate rooms in the house may be better than trying to ignore their fighting.

Whenever such a strategy is possible, it should be given serious consideration. Discovering effective consequences and designing practice are time-consuming tasks, so before you devote time to them, explore the possibility of making easy changes in the situation.

A new music teacher was told that the sixth graders should practice their parts in a song and not fool around with the guitars. But 20 guitars were lined against the wall! If only one were nudged all 20 would fall. Here is a rule and environment working together to guarantee punishment and very little singing. The sixth graders were to leave the piano alone too, but the cover to that was locked anyway. Good. No punishment for that today!

Of course, sixth graders must learn to follow rules without locks and keys but not 30 at a time with 20 guitars balanced against the wall and a new teacher to protect them. Gradual changes in an environment must be planned. The changes must begin with a situation that gives the advantage to the child. This chapter will describe how to set up those situations and how to adjust them gradually.

## Strategies for Success

Perhaps your strategy cannot guarantee the absence of bad behavior or the occurrence of good behavior. Still, you may be able to plan strategies that put the odds in your favor. For example, you may ensure that there will be more *opportunities* for good behavior. All mothers know that their children get cranky or tired at certain times. This fact must be taken into account when planning strategies concerned with a particular aggressive behavior. If a child is cranky before dinner and one of his problems is fighting with other children, then it seems reasonable to plan his day so that children do not visit him just before dinner. Another plan might be to have dinner at an earlier hour or lunch at a later hour. These alternatives are not strategies of consequences to control behavior but merely rearrangements of the family environment. Some rearrangements of this sort maximize the probabilities of good behavior and minimize the probabilities of bad behavior without the use of a new consequence.

For example, parents and teachers know that homework behavior can be improved with proper surroundings, and PTAs encourage parents to provide a "quiet and private place conducive to homework activities". It is important that these kinds of arrangements be thought of not only in terms of homework behavior, for there are a number of situations in which it is not possible or convenient or desirable to control direct, logical consequences, and we are limited to changing only the general environment.

Accidents at mealtime can be easily influenced by the way the situation is first set up. If a child is given a glass of milk and a glass of juice, three utensils when he uses only one, and five foods on his plate when he never even eats three, and he is then seated on two slippery telephone books, there are bound to be accidents. The goal may be to make him eat successfully under such circumstances, but initially a simpler task should be provided so that there is some chance of success and encouragement.

Consider also a child who refuses to eat his vegetables because he wants ice cream—and, given the choice, what healthy child would not prefer ice cream to beans? His parents might tell him that he can't have dessert unless he eats the "proper" foods first—not a bad approach, except that when parents come anywhere near an aversive or punishing procedure they usually begin to talk a lot. They threaten, they gibe, they insult before they finally withhold the dessert or get out the belt. They could carry through and deny the ice cream without having said a word during dinner, but usually the parents are so loving and so afraid that the child may have forgotten the rule that they begin with gentle reminders that quickly become nagging about food.

What changes in the environment can reduce poor eating habits in this situation? If the dessert-eating problem is considered serious enough, desserts could be eliminated entirely. If the child were hungry, he would have to eat what was there. There would be no arguing because there would be nothing to argue about. However, it would also mean that the parents too would be denied dessert. A less drastic procedure would be for the parents to have their dessert later, after the child has been put to bed. If such measures seem drastic in relationship to the seriousness of the problem, then perhaps the dinnertime unpleasantness about eating habits was also too extreme.

Perhaps while searching for a fair and effective consequence you'll discover that for your child it's best to put out what you want her to eat and follow it with a small dessert. Let resulting appetites determine eating at meals and don't beg or threaten. It's safer to let natural appetites influence food selection than to have the child use eating as an attention-getting device.

## Raising Expectations

When it is necessary to use a reward, some searching may help you find the best way to use it. To find the right consequence to use at the right time you must first ask, "What if he had done it right?" This should be one of the most frequent questions in the strategy session when the problem of a bad behavior, or the absence of a good one, comes up. Furthermore, before you can consider what the reaction will be when a good behavior occurs, you must find the situation in which the good behavior is most likely to occur.

In the mealtime-accident situation, the "environment" can be simplified, but the *rules* must be simplified as well. "Any use of the spoon will bring praise" might be the first rule. Here again it is necessary to begin at a basic-enough level to ensure that the child will be rewarded.

A more complicated problem involves a child who does not come home on time for dinner. Punishing consequences could be brought to bear by removing his dinner from the table, by letting the dinner get cold, by spanking him, or by limiting him to the house before dinnertime. These consequences would have some effect, but the situation might be set up so that there are positive reasons for coming home on time. Punishment answers the question "What if he does it wrong?" But what are the answers to such questions as "What if he does it right?" "What reasons have been provided for his returning home on time?" "What is there about the situation and the consequences that makes you believe that he *should* be responding 'correctly'?" It is within the framework of such questions that the inevitable consequences of coming home to dinner must be considered.

For most children, the reaction to their coming home is very predictable. At dinner questions are asked about how events have gone that day. Most teen-agers have learned to answer these questions with a very brief "OK" or just a shrug, if they can get away with it. They know which side their parents will be on if they discuss their teachers. If they have gotten into trouble, they know that sympathy is unlikely. The probability of verbal punishment is high, however, so it seems best to wait to talk to peers about such things, because the general probability of agreement and sympathy is much better. At times, parents do reward, encourage, and sympathize. But usually they have never stated, even between themselves, what specifically they want to encourage. Their encouragement is therefore inconsistent. It is hard for the teen-ager to predict just what the parents' mood is or what mood the teen-ager might touch off. It seems better to play it safe and shut up.

When moody or inconsistent parents do praise or reward some activity, they are not appreciated. The child knows their praise is more a product of a good mood than of his own activities. The lack of a thoughtful plan by the parents leads to erratic reactions and makes cynics out of children.

Any reward for coming home is made even less likely be-

---

## EXPERIMENT 18

### Parental Self-Modification

Frankie and Hannah[27] (age five) had been rejected from regular kindergarten class for many reasons including "hyperactivity". They were suspected of having serious physical and emotional problems. Their mothers had successfully used behavior modification techniques in improving mealtime, bedtime, and playtime behaviors. But they still attended to many bad behaviors and missed opportunities to reward good behaviors.

Observers conducted sessions for one hour each day, five days a week, for six months. The observer sat quietly on a small stool. She didn't speak to the mother or child after initially greeting them and telling the child, "I'm a worker now." Every ten seconds the observer recorded the occurrence of: inappropriate behavior of the child (breaking, throwing, damaging furniture, stealing food, screaming, kicking, pinching people or animals, etc.), annoying verbal habits, such as repeating the same phrase over and over, and parental attention ("un-huh", "good", "stop

that", grabbing, hitting, restraining the child, etc). Also, the order of occurrence of these behaviors was recorded.

After baseline observations, each mother was given a wrist counter and told to keep a running count of the times she gave attention to her child for good behavior. Praise, instruction, and hugging were given as some examples of attention. After counting attention for good behaviors the experimenter asked the mothers to stop counting for a few sessions. Then Hannah's mother was asked to count "wrong" attention (attention for bad behavior), and Frankie's mother was asked to go back to counting attention for good behavior.

In the final phase, both mothers were then asked to count attention for good behaviors, and then counting was faded out by removing it from some sessions. As you can see from the graphs in Figures 12 and 13, having the mothers pay attention to themselves resulted in better use of that attention. And, when the mothers watch how they parent, they not only improve, they stay improved!

cause the parents become more and more impatient. Their level of expectation (the behavior they are willing to reward) concerning how the child should act when he gets there is raised. This level *should* be determined by what the parents know the child will (not could) do. But it is likely that the expectation is determined more by the child's age than by his present ability.

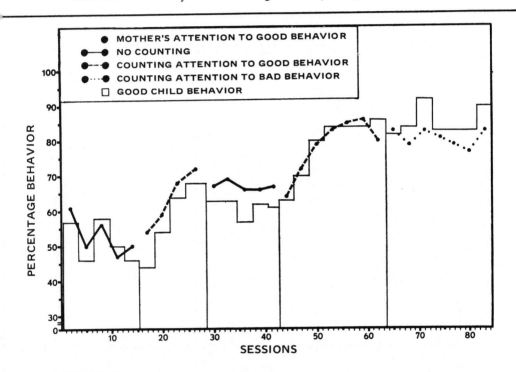

**FIGURE 12**

Percentage of maternal attention following appropriate behavior and the percentage of Frankie's behavior recorded as appropriate across no-counting and counting conditions.

(Adapted with permission of the **Journal of Applied Behavior Analysis.** Herbert, E.W., and Baer, D.M. "Training parents as behavior modifiers: Self-recording of contingent attention." **Journal of Applied Behavior Analysis.** 1972, 5, 144. Copyright 1972 by the Society for the Experimental Analysis of Behavior, Inc.)

This attitude ensures that he will fail the parents again and that he will be punished again. What does all this make of dinnertime? Something the child would just as soon be late for. When this has become the home atmosphere, it is time to look for new ways and new behaviors to reward.

When you consider your usual plan and attitude toward the

**FIGURE 13**

Percentage of maternal attention following appropriate behavior and the percentage of Hannah's behavior recorded as appropriate across conditions.

(Adapted with permission of the **Journal of Applied Behavior Analysis.** Herbert, E.W., and Baer, D.M. "Training parents as behavior modifiers: Self-recording of contingent attention." **Journal of Applied Behavior Analysis.** 1972, 5, 146. Copyright 1972 by the Society for the Experimental Analysis of Behavior, Inc.)

things your child says at dinnertime, just how inevitable are his rewards? Can he expect agreement and companionship at dinner or is it more realistic to expect disagreement and confrontation? If you find your answers to these questions uncomfortable, then possibly it is time to lower your standards and make your acceptance and agreement more plentiful.

## A System of Rewards

The availability of some rewards changes throughout the day. For example, parents may do a better job of supporting, encouraging, and giving social rewards early in the day. If this is true, perhaps the child should do his homework and clean up his room as soon as he returns from school, rather than after dinner. In the earlier part of the day circumstances are favorable; the child and parents are not as tired as they will be later. Therefore, the probabilities of the child's good behavior and the parents' rewards are both high.

Needless to say, the probabilities of parents' good behavior depend on circumstances also. For parents the good behaviors are those that successfully and efficiently support the correct performance of their children. So select and develop situations in which you have a high probability of acting correctly. The probability will be influenced not only by the time of day but also by the consequences you select. By planning a convenient consequence, you can determine that it will be used. For example, setting up a penny bank, candy jar, or convenient tally sheet in your kitchen may make your use of rewards more efficient. It will also make rewards more available and obvious to your child.

Social consequences such as attention are the easiest to use because they are the most convenient. A person needs only himself, no paraphernalia, to use these rewards. Such social consequences can be less obvious, however. Therefore, they are less effective, and in most cases their use is not well planned.

No one can or would want to control all his reactions to his child, but some control is necessary. When you think your control is needed, make sure you select a consequence you really *can* control. Your control over the use of some consequences varies—for example, TV time can be used as a positive consequence for completing homework assignments and other good behaviors or as a punishment when it is removed for some bad behavior. Using TV time as a reward may be effective at times and ineffective at others, because the appeal of a TV program to your child varies during the day. Also, you do not control what TV program will be on when you want to use it as a consequence. To avoid these complications you may want to use the tally sheet to increase or decrease TV time allotted and then allow the child to choose when he will cash in some of that time. This procedure solves the problem of what time good programs are on, but it lacks the characteristic of an immediate consequence. Therefore, a social reward should be given when a good mark is made on the tally sheet in order to emphasize the reward at the right time.

A tally sheet has many advantages in controlling consequences such as time privileges. It can be used to control allowance, outdoor play, or any other measurable privilege that might well be controlled for the sake of the child's behavior.

When privileges are to be controlled, it is important to build rules about minimums and maximums that you know you can stick to. Do not set up extremes that will "really fix" your child or "make him stand up and take notice." Set your standards so that with an easy conscience you can apply the consequence immediately and consistently over a long period of time. You might wish to set a minimum amount of TV time per day at a half-hour and a maximum at an hour and a half. That way, the total tally of the child's good behavior or bad behavior cannot create a ridiculous situation. If you use fifteen-minute intervals as a reward, you have as many as six concrete encouragements that can be given each day for some desirable activity.

For preschool and grade-school children, consider making constant use of social attention that involves various types of physical affection. In grade-school classes it is very effective for the teacher merely to walk around patting the shoulder of a child who is making an effort. Sometimes no words are necessary, nor are they as beneficial as a smile and a pat. These gestures lack directness; they don't *tell* the child what is being praised, and they can be used indiscriminately. Nevertheless, they can be extremely effective with small children you love and want to plan for and work to help.

It is very useful to record the number of times you give physical rewards, supports, and encouragements, for you will gain information about the frequencies of your own good behaviors as well as useful information about your child's good behaviors. Begin to take advantage of recording, in a rather rigorous way, when things happen.

### Fashioning the Ideal

In the process of making rewards inevitable, you often have to settle at first for behavior that is less than ideal. You must taper the ideal to what the child can and will do in the beginning, so that the rule allows reward for a low-level response. But there has to be a plan for a gradual change of the rule under which rewards occur. There are two possibilities: you can expand the requests or you can expand the range of circumstances. Expanding the request, asking for even better behaviors, is called shaping. Expanding the range of circumstances where the *same behavior* will be asked for and rewarded is called fading. The distinction is important, because no new behavioral definitions are needed for fading, whereas a new and better behavior is needed for shaping. The following example will point out these differences.

The mother of a child who would not talk in school sought help from a counselor. Her daughter would speak at home but never say a word in school. Promotion from first grade was dependent on demonstrating reading ability by reading aloud. There was no need for shaping behavior, however. The behavior was already learned under one circumstance (the home). To help the child, situations were arranged that were increasingly similar to the classroom. First, the mother met the child in the classroom after school. The daughter would sit in her seat and read aloud to

## EXPERIMENT 19

### Fading and Shaping

Twelve four- and five-year-old children[28] of the Robin Bird Nursery School were going to learn to read their first words. The words were shown to each child individually by "Happy the Clown", a face on a slide projector screen.

The children were asked to tell Happy the words as they were presented on slides. Each slide also had a picture representing the word (i.e., apple, ball, horse, dog, elephant, or book). Each time the children were correct Happy's nose would light up, and occasionally a mechanism would give them candy. The words were all presented six times. However, for half of the children the helping picture slowly faded out of view as the slides continued to be presented. The other six children saw the helping picture clearly until the last presentation when the pictures were abruptly absent.

On the last presentation when the pictures had been removed for all twelve children, those who had had the pictures faded out over preceding trials showed near-

ly perfect word identification. Those who merely had the pictures removed for this last test could only average one out of six correct word identifications.

In another study on fading, five heavy cigarette smokers[29] used a special cigarette pack resembling the one that shocked the smokers in Experiment 8. However, in this procedure every time a cigarette was removed from the case the lid remained locked for a pre-set length of time. Over a period of weeks, the amount of time the case was locked was gradually increased by the experimenter's adjusting the timing mechanism. As Figure 14 shows the number of cigarettes smoked decreased as the time between cigarettes was forcibly extended by the timing mechanism on the case. Subjects were also asked to observe each other to see if more than one cigarette was removed at a time. They also checked on each other's borrowing. The subjects reported only four cases of borrowing and no instances of removing more than one cigarette at a time.

her mother with no one else present. Later, as the fading procedure was developed, the teacher stayed in the room during these
sessions but remained busy with her own work and took no
notice of the mother-and-daughter reading session. As the days
went by, the teacher took more and more notice. Finally, she did
nothing but look at the girl and listen to her read. In the last

**FIGURE 14**

Cigarette smoking in subjects with the locked cigarette case.

(Adapted with permission of the **Journal of Applied Behavior Analysis.** Azrin,
N.H., and Powell, J. "Behavioral engineering: The reduction of smoking behavior
by a conditioning apparatus and procedure." **Journal of Applied Behavior Analysis.** 1968, 1, 196. Copyright 1968 by the Society for the Experimental Analysis
of Behavior, Inc.)

sessions the mother sat farther away and the teacher sat nearer. At last the sessions were held before the other students left the classroom.

The fading procedure just described did not require that new behaviors be learned. If it had been necessary to teach the child to read, the problem would have been magnified. New behaviors would have been shaped and definitions of these new behaviors would have been required. The initial, low level of behavior may have been identifying pictures or letters. Later, simple words would have been added to the lesson, and so on.

Whenever you are using a shaping process, then, you must begin with some level of behavior that occurs frequently, so that the child can learn rules and experience the reality of rewards right away. Even at this level, the child should be told that later the rules will change. Tell the child the direction of the change and when it will take place. Also, you must be prepared to pay off in some way for a long period of time after you reach some acceptable level of performance. During this time do not be afraid to backtrack, even below the first level of behavior you asked for. The idea behind the shaping process is to keep the rules lenient enough so that the rewards occur, but only as a result of the stated rule. Do not take leniency in shaping to mean that any old behavior will do or that a few free ones now and then will not hurt—they will. There is reason and consistency in the behavior of the child. Therefore, do not be concerned about using simple rules that are easy for the child. They can eventually be shaped upward.

In nearly every case the ideal behavior is not gained in one easy step. At first you will have to dig back to some low level of behavior that can guarantee that some opportunities will be available for rewards. After this initial level of performance has been strengthened, the next level of performance will also have to be somewhat short of the final goal. It is a matter of shaping a behavior up from a lower level of performance; it is a gradual process. The gradual process must not tempt you to ignore an explicit definition of the next levels, however. Lack of such definitions certainly will lead you into an inconsistent use of the reward.

Once some new level of performance has been attained, the problem is how fast the child can be moved along. Of course, there will be individual differences in this kind of learning, as in any other. The temptation is to adopt a rule that says you can never move too slowly. Nevertheless, the feedback for successful performance is always a factor in reward, and feedback for the same old performance can go stale if you don't move on to reward some new and better approximation of the long-range goal. Also, dwelling on one stage may make it difficult to move along later. Consider the parent who praises baby talk. This is a necessary first stage in the shaping of talking, but as this level is prolonged, many developments can become troublesome. The longer the child continues baby talk, the more likely he is to respond to the discovery that some people (grandmothers, grandfathers, aunts, and uncles) will always praise this level of performance. Also, the longer the child continues baby talk, the more likely it is that his parents will understand it and, therefore, inadvertently reward it. And the longer the child continues baby talk, the more likely it is that it will become an attention-getting device. These complications have their counterparts in eating, dressing, and many other training situations.

There is a better rule than the one that says you can never move too slowly. It says, "When in doubt, move up for a while but keep in mind that it is all right to go back a step if necessary."

One of the most common reasons for hesitating to move up is that the next step involves some real consequences for the parents. After a child has learned to count money and make change, he is ready to do some shopping—probably with your money. This is a very dangerous time for hesitation on your part, because this is when the child learns whether these things are really useful and meaningful to him. You cannot expect him to be eager about your instruction (or the school's instruction) if the reason for his effort is supposed to be "Someday you'll need to know these things." Make him "need to know these things" now.

✎ In the later stages of shaping, the parent's role changes. The parent has shaped the child and prepared him for the next steps, but the world provides more and more of the consequences. At this point, the quality of the job that the parents do can be judged by noting how realistic and practical the training was. But there is still a parental duty. Even though parents give a smaller proportion of the consequences as a child grows up, as observers they still have an obligation to point out why certain consequences occur—why certain behaviors are successful and others are not.

The crucial point to remember is that this change of duty does not happen at a particular age or even at a particular age for a particular child. It happens at different times for different behaviors. Hopefully, you will finish giving planned and contrived rewards for toilet training by six, for eating behavior by eight or ten, and for money training by twelve, but you may still be working on social behavior with friends at eighteen. When and how to encourage and support behaviors in social situations is a continual learning process for all of us.

## Check List for Action

In Part I we have laid the groundwork for the types of strategies that you can develop to solve many of the problems of parenthood. Before we turn to the special problems of children, teenagers, and the family, however, let us briefly review the questions that you should ask yourself before you put these strategies into practice.

*Is the problem big enough to bother with?* Remember that even a "No" here should indicate a strategy. The strategy may be merely to eliminate nagging about the problem.

*Am I attempting too much at one time?* If you begin to

believe in consequential control, the biggest danger is that you will try too many things at once. Don't attempt to control eating, piano practicing, bed making, and homework all at once. Concentrating on too many activities not only makes it more likely that you will make errors but also creates confusion about rules for the child, even if your errors are low. Think small. Begin with one rule at a time.

*Can the behavior be guaranteed without the management of consequences?* Some behaviors can be made impossible, and that strategy is sometimes easier than using rules. As noted earlier, in these cases you can change the behavior by changing the situation in which it occurs.

*If consequences are to be used, has a clear behavioral definition been worked out to signal when consequences will and will not be used?* If the answer here is "No," consider defining just one part of the many activities that make up the problem—for example, instead of "neatly dressed," just "shoe tying"; instead of "fighting with brothers," just "fighting with one brother"; instead of "never minding," just "coming when called for dinner."

*Have the reasons (current consequences) been carefully identified?* If the answer is difficult, perhaps you haven't looked far enough. Possibly some chain or group of behaviors is performed before the consequence occurs. For example, complaining about school only results in the parents' suggestion of what to do about homework, which then gives opportunity for procrastinating about it and then parental attention. The complaint is a secondary means to the child's goal—a step along the way. Consider the child who fights and complains with his siblings in order to get the parent to interfere, in order that they can be separated, in order that he can have a room to himself. Parental attention here is only a step along the way.

*Can the behavior be made more probable by providing some changes in the training?* The answer concerns the necessities for the performance of the behavior. For example, if the child is to learn to come home on time, does he have a watch? If he is to learn to eat correctly without spilling things, does he have a chair of the correct height? Give the child the best situation you can.

*Am I starting with a behavior that is simple enough so that I am sure that rewards can occur—even on the first day?*

*Are the rewards handy?* Is there a pencil next to your allowance chart? Will you be available to give encouragement at homework time?

*If rewards are to be removed for bad behavior, has the resulting deprivation been prepared for?* If tantrums are to be ignored, what is to be attended?

*What are the fading and/or shaping levels?* The first level of shaping will have been dealt with under behavioral definitions, and the first situation from which fading might occur will have been determined by the selection of a time and place for the first practice. The small changes in the rules that allow practice to be expanded from these first circumstances should be just as well planned as the first rules.

## OBJECTIVES    *chapter six*    — 2, 5, 6, 7

1.   What is overcorrection?

2.   Give two reasons why punishment
     can come to serve as a reward.

3.   What is the advantage of planning
     the conditions of practice as well as
     the consequences?

4.   When privileges are to be used as con-
     sequences, why is it important to
     develop realistic rules about maxi-
     mums and minimums?

5.   Define fading.  Define shaping.
     What is the difference between
     fading and shaping?

6.   State the rule about the speed with
     which shaping should progress.

7.   How does the parents' role in the
     early stages of shaping differ from
     their role in later stages?

# Part II
# BLUEPRINTS
# FOR CHANGE

# 7 / *Early Social Problems*

The first signs of problems in relating to others usually shows up at playtime. Somehow the situation produces aggression, non-cooperation, and fussing (at everybody). Try to focus on the situation and the reactions the child is getting. Avoid focusing on the child's "sick personality". It may be that the child brings the results of some bad past experiences into the situation (sick personality) but we can't turn back the calendar. So let's go ahead from here.

As usual, the first few "trials" in a new situation are crucial. Set the cards in your favor. Pick times when he is well rested, well fed, and feeling good. It would be unfortunate if the first experiences were at a day-care center where he is freshly deserted by his mother, thrust into a group where he and other strange children outnumber the adults 10 or 20 to 1, with two hours to go 'til juice time! Things are already looking bad when that first kid comes up to grab your security toy.

If a day-care or Sunday school experience is in your child's future, let the first extended social situations be earlier when he has a better chance. When he first goes over to play with the neighbor's child be there for support and well-timed encouragements for good behaviors. Also provide one or both of the following advantages: *semi-structured activity and/or modeling.*

The time when you are most likely to have play problems with small children (or teen-agers) is when there is no specific task to be performed. This does not mean that you have to play camp counselor or teacher whenever your children are playing with other children. But you should recognize your solution to the play problem as being one in which you must suggest or provide some new opportunities for new things to do rather than one in which you must reprimand poor social behavior.

The procedure of copying someone's behavior is called *modeling* or imitation. Although it is a simple idea, many people forget that their attempts to control others are also behaviors that their children may copy. This is one way an adult's disposition and resulting social problems (play problems) get passed along to the children. How do you handle your social behavior toward others? How do you handle your social problems with this child? Set a good example in these play situations. An adult (teacher, parent, or camp counselor) can't expect the children to use reward and tolerance if the adult handles problems with strict rules backed by punishment!

## Sociability

Being sociable is like many other activities: If you are good at it, you like it and you tend to do more of it. On the other hand, if you fail to get along with others, then you probably don't like being with others and tend to do very little socializing.

A child who is good at socializing has many friends. These friends agree to do what he wants to do, laugh at the things he thinks are funny, and cooperate and play games he likes to play. They don't seem to try to please each other; they just do. The notion of being pleasing in order to make friends seems too simple to be of any use until pleasing, agreeing, and cooperating are seen as special cases of reward and punishment. Consider, for example, the following conversation, which took place at a table where three first-graders were working on pictures:

EDDIE [*Pokes Tom.*]:    Don't do it like that, dum-dum!

TOM:    Leave me alone!

JON:    Give me the yellow.

EDDIE [*Reaches for the yellow crayon and pulls it close to himself.*]:    I need it now.

TEACHER:    Give Jon the yellow crayon.

[*Eddie throws the yellow crayon at Jon. Later he turns to Jon.*]

EDDIE:    Are you through with the yellow now?

JON:    Yes.

[*As Jon starts to hand over the yellow crayon, Eddie grabs Jon's hand and digs out the crayon.*]

What happened during this art lesson? First, Eddie punished Tom ("Don't do it like that, dum-dum!"). Second, Tom tried to punish Eddie ("Leave me alone!"). Third, Eddie refused Jon's request for the yellow crayon and later added another punishment by snatching it back when Jon offered it. Eddie was a punisher. He looked for bad things to punish. If he did not find them, he punished good things (for example, Jon's offer of the crayon). The best way to avoid punishment from Eddie—perhaps the only way—was to avoid Eddie.

For Eddie to change he had to learn how to reward, and to learn this, someone had to reward Eddie for rewarding others. Also, he needed a good example set for him, and his parents could try to do that. If it worked and was a rewarding effort for them, then they, too, might benefit and learn some new ways of living! This strategy had to begin at home. In Eddie's case his parents needed retraining in the use of rewards and punishments also. His mother had to learn to watch for Eddie's rewarding behavior—she had to be a coach in this social game.

Eddie's mother also had to provide as little attention as possible when Eddie punished. If he used verbal punishment, she ignored it; if he used physical punishment, she paid him just enough attention to shut him off by himself. When his parents began to use some reward rules, Eddie's behavior got better. He had some pleasant attention to work for at home, and he even began to show that he believed he could create some pleasant attention for himself at school.

GANGS / Most children develop some very close friends who are extremely influential on their behavior. If there are only one or two friends at a time, they are called bosom buddies; several friends form a clique; a very large group is usually thought of as a gang.

The word "gang" frightens the adult because it describes a group that adheres to its own set of rules rather than to the ones that the rest of us agree upon. A gang of teen-agers does not spurn all rules, but they have come to live, at least partly, by a set

## EXPERIMENT 20

### Peer Reward

Ricky, Dennis, Tim and Lisa[30] were first graders who talked, walked around the classroom, or just "day dreamed" during study times. John, a fifth grader, took the job of observing these children and providing good consequences for good behavior. He watched the four children each day when they were to be working on an assignment while the teacher was busy with a reading group. Whenever he observed a child doing the assigned task, John pushed a switch on a small panel before him. He had a separate switch for each child and when it was in the "on"

position it ran a clock.

John found that all four children worked less than 50% of the time (see "baseline" in the lefthand part of the graph in Figure 15).

In the next phase of John's experiment a light was placed on each of the children's desks. Ricky's and Dennis' light worked whenever John was running their "good behavior clock". John also continued to time Tim's and Lisa's good behavior but without activating their lights.

In the third phase the lights were activated for everybody. Ricky and Dennis were also given special tickets (which of rules that they themselves devise. They support these rules through their own social rewards and punishments. Usually, they are more successful than their parents in shaping behavior, because parents ordinarily give their social rewards rather freely out of love and do not adhere to a strict set of rules. Also, the overall social reward given by the members of the gang may be larger than the overall social reward given by parents.

The gang gives more reward because usually parents have rules and definitions only about bad behaviors that the child might perform and therefore have programs only for dispensing punishments (dispensing rewards out of love requires no rules). The gang, on the other hand, has a fairly precise notion about what good behavior is and rewards it well. If you find yourself in competition with your child's "gang," you might improve your position in that competition by being more rewarding and by

could be used for gym or playground time or other special privileges) if they showed enough "good behavior time". First, they needed only two good behavior minutes in the 20-minute session. This was eventually increased to 19 minutes — 95% — of good behavior time.

Only in the fourth phase did Tim and Lisa also get the special tickets. In the middle of the graph in Figure 15 you see almost perfect performance when John was giving both light and tickets as a consequence.

In the next phase light and tickets were given for time spent **not** working! Although the behavior decreased to nearly zero, it quickly recovered when the old rules were put back into effect. This reverse in the rules shows that just giving privileges is not enough. The reward must reliably follow the good behavior.

John checked up on his subjects more than a month after the end of the experiment. He first observed them secretly via a remote TV picture taken by a hidden camera. Then he went back into the room to time behaviors once more. The children's almost perfect performance at the far right of the graph shows that they still remembered and performed for him!

**FIGURE 15**

Good behavior as a function of John's strategies.

(Adapted with permission of the **Journal of Applied Behavior Analysis.** Surratt, P.R., Ulrich, R.E., and Hawkins, R.P. "An elementary student as a behavioral engineer." **Journal of Applied Behavior Analysis.** 1969, 2, 88. Copyright 1969 by the Society for the Experimental Analysis of Behavior, Inc.)

rewarding by a set of rules that specify the good behaviors.

JEALOUSY AND FIGHTING / Aggression between siblings over parental rewards frequently takes the form of jealousy and fighting. Such emotionality occurs partly because of the lack of rewards (attention, and so on) and partly because of the lack of rules about rewards (that is, disposition). If the child does not know the rules, he finds himself unable to control the amount of social attention he gets. He is responding to the fact that some of the rules are arbitrary, random, and unplanned. Whether he or his brother or his sister gets the most attention does not seem to depend upon any specific rule that defines the good behaviors. The only rule that seems to be applied consistently is that the sibling whose bad behavior attracts attention is likely to get the most time with his parents.

Attention for bad behaviors seems aversive and is meant to be punitive. It still counts as attention, however, and has the added joy of keeping attention away from the other children in the family. So it can be helpful to see excessive jealousy as an outgrowth of procedures that support bad behavior.

Of course, the groundwork for such a situation is often laid by an overall lack of positive social attention from the parents. When there is little reward to be had, there will be a great deal of fighting over the little scraps of reward that filter down from the parents.

Fighting differs from jealous behavior because the lack of rules is much less a factor in maintaining the fighting behavior. The fighting behavior is more specifically supported by lack of attention, and the strategy usually indicated is very similar to that which would be applied in the case of tantrums when attention is added for good behavior (see Chapter 8).

THE ONLY CHILD / The behavioral development of an only child is usually directed by a small, strict set of rules more appropriate to the adults in the family than to the child. The child acts very grown up but has many play problems because he lacks training in sociability with children of his own age. Because the rules are strict, the opportunities for practice with children without interference from the parents are few. Therefore, the parents of an only child should encourage long play sessions with other children without interfering.

Long uninterrupted play sessions are doubly important for the only child because playmates usually provide a more demanding set of social rules. These rules will be in healthy contrast to those of the only child's parents, who are likely to be too lenient concerning aggression, too indulgent of demands, and too compliant when a conflict appears over what activities will be done. For example, a mother was observed arguing with her daughter (an only child), who was angry because another child would not do things her way. The mother said, "You have to do things

## EXPERIMENT 21

### The Shoe on the Other Foot

Mrs. Z[31], a teacher, was asked to imagine a scale from zero to 100. She was asked to picture 100 as the score given to the most irritating student she could think of. Zero represented a student who caused no trouble. Using these guidelines, she assigned a number to each student she had in her class.

From these results and further comments by Mrs. Z and the principal, Robin and Karen were selected by the experimenter to help change Mrs. Z's behavior. Robin was eleven and was one of the worst behavior problems in the school.

He was sent to the principal's office almost every day. Karen, also eleven, had a similar reputation and a very high rating on the disruptive behavior scale.

Mrs. Z was asked to make two lists of classroom behaviors — inappropriate, and appropriate. She listed appropriate behaviors as following instructions, paying attention, having necessary materials, raising hands rather than talking out. Inappropriate behaviors, Mrs. Z defined as talking back, touching items in or on the teacher's desk, being out-of-seat, talking out, and inattention.

Observers counted all of these behaviors and teacher reactions as well. The teacher's reactions were divided into praise,

Jane's way sometimes, or she won't want to play with you anymore." "But," said the daugher, "she won't let me have the toy and she won't do it right!" The mother replied, "Well, let me get you another toy to play with," and she did.

The daughter wanted to be boss again. The other child was willing to apply a consequence to this demand and, in effect, say that if she was going to be bossy, she couldn't play—probably a good lesson for the child to learn. Her mother "saved" the daughter from this lesson, however, by getting involved. The mother provided an alternative that would not demand that her daughter learn to compromise with others.

In this instance the daughter would have gained more if her mother had not interfered. The mother tried to rectify a difficult situation in which her daughter didn't have her very own way, but in the process her daughter lost an opportunity to learn how much it costs to be bossy. As a matter of fact, the daughter

---

reprimands, neutral remarks and instructions.

The appropriate behaviors of both the students and Mrs. Z were low throughout baseline (see Figure 16). The situation remained poor even when the students were instructed outside of class on just how to perform for observers (see the second part of the graph in Figure 16). However, when rewards (model car kits for Robin and phonograph records for Karen) were offered for each two-day period in which less than two inappropriate behaviors occurred, the students' behavior improved.

Mrs. Z's behavior also showed great improvement even though she had no knowledge that she was being observed, nor that particular students were being coached.

When Robin was told the experiment was over and rewards were discontinued, his appropriate behaviors dropped 50%, but Mrs. Z's appropriate behavior dropped 100%! Her behavior with Karen remained good while Karen remained good. Who's controlling whom?

Of course, the answer is that teachers control students some of the time and, students control teachers some of the time. And each can do better with a little help from the other.

**FIGURE 16**
Percent of Robin's and Karen's appropriate behavior and the teacher's behavior
in using consequences.

(Adapted with permission of the **Journal of Applied Behavior Analysis.** Sherman,
T.M., and Cormier, W.H. "An investigation of the influence of student behavior
on teacher behavior." **Journal of Applied Behavior Analysis.** 1974, 7, 16. Copyright 1974 by the Society for the Experimental Analysis of Behavior, Inc.)

learned a new way to get the mother's attention *and* to have a social situation arranged for her.

The best strategy here is for the parents to do what they can to bring their child into long periods of contact with other children. Providing transportation and opportunity for such sessions will be time well spent. If, in addition to this strategy, the parents can plan carefully what to do when other attention-getting behaviors come up, then the only-child problem will get better.

## Rules Are Made to be Broken?

Rules with positive consequences are rules that challenge a child to be successful. Only rules with negative consequences risk being broken for the sake of "beating" the parent or teacher.

Of course, whenever a rule is laid down by parents, sooner or later a child must test it to see if the parents meant what they said. Rule-testing behavior is learned just as any other behavior is learned. It comes from the child's past experiences with the way his parents follow through on their rules. A mother who complains that her child is testing her every time she sets up a new rule should first consider how often she changes her mind as a result of being tested, or makes a challenging and rewarding experience out of the adventure of testing the rule. Fathers seem particularly vulnerable to making parenting a child competitive. Save the healthy competition for games and leave "winning" out of behavioral rules.

Rule testing occurs when the child fails to measure up (on purpose or by failure). It becomes a moment of truth for the adult. Here's where the adult gives real practice if the rewards (and punishments, if any) are fair and reasonable. For only if they are fair and reasonable can the adult carry through and have the child progress. If the rules are too strict, unmanageable, not consistent, the children will still learn something—they learn to look for loopholes in rules!

Of course, there will always be some looking for loopholes, and the child needs these tests as practice and experience. If one had only to state a rule for it to be obeyed, consequences would be unnecessary. Rule testing becomes a problem only if parents are unsure of whether or not they want to enforce the rule or if they have created a rule so difficult for the child that he makes a great many errors and ends in failure.

If failure, testing, and loophole searching are a problem, ask yourself two questions: "Is the rule testing occurring because he really can't measure up to the rule?" and "Is the rule testing occurring because I have not yet decided how to enforce the rule?" If the answer to either question is "yes," then further strategy sessions are necessary. These sessions should be devoted to making a simpler rule, a rule that guarantees more success so that you can feel comfortable carrying out that enforcement.

Another version of rule testing is complaining. It is a search for the possible loophole in the rule or for the times when the rule can be overcome. If you are a victim of complaining, then it is time to review your rules and see why at times you can be persuaded to refrain from enforcing them. The most common reason is that there are too many rules to enforce. Or possibly there is something about the rules you have that could be changed so that you can feel more comfortable in enforcing them consistently and therefore be less vulnerable to complaints. Again, the strategy session can help you review the number and kinds of rules you are enforcing.

There is one respect in which the complaining behavior is not rule-testing behavior. At times complaining can be actively supported by parents who are willing to do a lot of arguing—particularly if the parents feel unsure of the fairness of the rule to begin with. Lack of confidence in your own rules may make you feel obliged to defend them verbally. This defense is fun for the children and in fact provides a reward for complaining. So even if you continue to enforce the rule and do not give in, the argument itself may still continue the complaining behavior.

## School Behavior

Before we consider what a parent can do to help his child in school, let us look at what is happening in the school with respect to behaviors and consequences for behaviors.

Where are the consequences, the results, for good schoolroom behavior? They certainly must exist, because most children perform at a fairly reliable and acceptable level. Students seem to be responsive to the rather infrequent encouragements from both parents and teachers, and they seem to gain encouragement from their own successes. But there are children who do not continue to perform for these more subtle rewards.

Sometimes it is argued that if good children can perform well under these circumstances, then problem children should also. This argument implies that problem children can make an abrupt change in performance and maintain that change in spite of the fact that they have not been able to do so in the past. The proponents of this argument tend to fall back on coercions, reprimands, and threats as the means of bringing about this change. Most of us have learned the painful lesson that they don't work.

In addition to some lack of encouragement for good behaviors in the school, there is sometimes a lack of good definitions of the behaviors to be encouraged. When the behavioral definitions are precise and concrete and the consequences are consistent, the procedures are usually efficient and successful. For example, teachers agree that the criterion for successful performance in first grade is that the child be able to read (easily defined), to recite the alphabet, and to do simple arithmetic. Because of this agreement, first-grade teachers know what to reward; they know what success is. Inadvertently, they may reward attention-getting behavior in problem children, but at least the teachers know what kind of work they want. But in the higher grades, the criterion for successful performance becomes increasingly vague, and, as a result, innovative techniques can go out of style because there is no general agreement on what the purpose (behavioral goal) of a new technique should be. What, precisely, should a sixth-grader be able to do in order to pass? Few people can agree.

At this point the school finds it difficult to be precise about behavior, and because of the number of students it falls back upon paper-and-pencil tests, which probe and sample the kind of information that a school board has determined a child should have at a given level. Unfortunately, a determination through a paper-and-pencil test cannot be done often enough or precisely enough for consequences to be used in an efficient way.

Because the definitions of good behaviors and behavioral goals are scarce at higher grades, teachers find themselves doing more and more of the classroom activities and students find themselves doing less and less. Thus, in kindergarten and first grade the teacher guides the painting, writing, adding, and subtracting while the students explore correct behaviors. But in college, the professor guides very little behavior and talks a great deal, while the students remain silent and inactive.

Learning by doing is generally considered a superior principle for the lower-grade school levels, but somehow this rule of practice is gradually discarded in higher grades. If the teacher and the parent lose the disposition to reward the student frequently because they do not know what, precisely, to reward, the student may lose direction. Consequently, many teachers construct their own projects for the children so that they can experience (usually only once) doing some things. Beyond the general goal of experience no specific goals hold the purposes of such projects together.

How can you, the parent, help a child who is performing poorly in this situation? If you decide that a low-performing child should do better in school, then you will just harp and nag. You must determine specific behaviors. These definitions will help you to plan what will be practiced and what will be learned.

First, determine some positive consequence that you can control and use it as a reward for effort—TV time, money, free time outside, special privileges. Second, specify a time and place, free of family interruptions, to work with your child. Third, go back to his classroom and homework papers of the last three months and ask him to correct these papers as your first behavioral definition. Fourth, pay off handsomely for each paper corrected; stay with your child and pay off with attention and admiration for individual items that he corrects on these pages. Fifth, keep these sessions short. Do not continue until the child looks tired or bored. Stop while he is still willing to work. Do not try to get all you can out of him at a session. It will only mean that there will be nothing left in him when you try to start the next session. If he suggests stopping before you do, you have waited too long. Sixth, keep a tally sheet in front of you during the session. Record the concrete rewards for him to see. Seventh, call his teacher and ask her to review these corrections in front of him when he brings them in.

The object of going back three months and of keeping the sessions short is to ensure a high probability of success and reward. The object of the other steps is to ensure that the reward occurs when the success occurs.

HOMEWORK / Like the other school behaviors discussed above, homework behavior is difficult to maintain because the direct consequences associated with the behavior occur somewhere off in the future, at school. The only immediate consequence of homework may be the loss of free time at home. The first question to ask is what positive consequence could be brought to bear on the homework behavior. You might consider some aspect of the token economy, described in Chapter 11, in which points or tokens could be given for a specified amount of homework time or a specified amount of homework completed. There are advantages to such a method, because it allows the parents to stop paying attention to, and thus supporting, the procrastination that usually complicates such a situation.

In addition to the short-range tangible rewards, some process will have to tell the child what is important about doing homework. The school has devised projects, experiments, and field trips to convince him that the things he is studying in school and at home are really important and respected in the outside world. But it is important that you, the parent, provide experiences and

*EXPERIMENT 22*

*"Good Behavior Games"*

The "good behavior game"[32] was introduced in Mrs. G's fourth grade class because of troublesome behavior. Seven students were frequently sent to the principal for scolding and there was general disruptive behavior among the rest of the students.

Two disruptive behaviors were counted by observers: out-of-seat behavior (including scooting around with the desk as well as leaving the assigned seat, standing or kneeling on the desk, and assuming other peculiar postures); talking-out behavior (including whispering, making animal sounds, howls, cat calls as well as just talking without permission).

Just after reading period one day, prior to math, Mrs. G announced, "During math period every day we will play a new game." She then divided the class into two teams and explained eleven rules concerning the two categories of disruptive behavior. These rules included no sitting on or moving desks, no traveling, no talk-

ing without permission, etc. She cautioned that whenever she observed someone breaking a rule his or her team would receive a mark on the chalk board. The team with the fewest marks would wear the victory tags, get to put a star by each team-member's name on the winner's chart, line up first for lunch, and take part in special free time activities during the last 30 minutes of the day.

If a team received no more than five marks, it was an automatic win. Sometimes both teams won this way. And, if less than 20 marks were obtained in a week, the team went to recess four minutes early next week.

Mrs. G's remark about applying the good behavior game to math was changed from time to time. Figure 17 shows disruptive behaviors for 21 sessions prior to the game. Then it shows the behaviors while she used the game only in math (sessions 22 to 44), and then when things were reversed, and then when she applied the game only to reading, and then to both. A 75% decrease in bad behavior with just a game!

**FIGURE 17**
Percent of time in which bad behavior occurred during different "games".

(Reprinted with permission of the **Journal of Applied Behavior Analysis.** Barrish, H.H., Saunder, M. and Wolf, M.M. "Good behavior game: Effects of individual contingencies for group consequences on disruptive behavior in the classroom." **Journal of Applied Behavior Analysis.** 1969, 2, 122. Copyright 1969 by the Society for the Experimental Analysis of Behavior, Inc.)

responsibilities that point out to the child, here and now, the usefulness of the things he is learning. Certainly a ten- or twelve-year-old can handle a checking account for the family or plan and carry out the food shopping for the family. This may necessarily involve a process in which you allow the child the responsibility of performing a task before he has the tools to do it. For example, you may assign to a child the responsibility of doing the checking account and collecting a "service charge." But when he sits down to do it, he may find that he does not know decimals and may say to you, "I can't do this because I don't know decimals," at which time you can say, "Oh, you need to know decimals. Let me show you how that's done." He might not enjoy the process of learning decimals any more than before, but at least he now has some concrete experience of why it is important and useful to learn about them, and when he does learn, he will be able to collect "service charges." When he is again seated in front of the bank statement, he may say, "I don't seem to be able to calculate percentages," at which time you can teach something about percentages to a child who now knows why he should learn them. Such a procedure sets out in front of the subject the ultimate goal, thus providing a motivation. Then it teaches the individual skills that he must have to perform that goal.

HOSTILITY TOWARD SCHOOL / A child is unhappy if he does poorly in school. People are usually unhappy about things they do not do well. Generally, the people who like golf are the people who play it well. One usually likes chess or bridge only if he is reasonably good at it.

If your child is unhappy in school and you begin with only a general and vague characteristic, his unhappiness, it will be difficult for you to find a behavior to be practiced and learned. But if you begin with some of the child's behaviors, then the situation doesn't seem so impossible. What are these behaviors? In school, they include answering arithmetic problems correctly, spelling words correctly, and writing in a legible hand. At home, they are the same activities applied to homework papers and assignments.

Now is the time to ask, "What happens next?" You are asking now for the consequences, the results, the events that happen after the good behavior occurs. When the child gives the correct spelling for a word on a spelling list at home or in school, little positive feedback occurs—especially if he is three weeks (or months) late in giving it. But now that you are dealing with more precise things than his unhappiness and his inability and his lack of desire, you can explore with him what might be rewarding and supportive of these good behaviors.

Because you are stating questions in behavioral terms, the strategy by which these behaviors can be shaped up becomes more evident. The father wants more money or praise from his boss, for example, and the mother wants praise and other kinds of social acceptance from her husband and her friends. The important question posed by the school problem is "What does the child want?" He would certainly like to have some verbal praise and acceptance, and some money and other tangible rewards. Then why does he respond so poorly? The answer lies in the relationship between what he gets and what he does. In his father's case, there is no doubt that job performance is related to the attitude of the boss. In his mother's case, there is also a definite relationship between her performance and other pleasant social events. But how about the child? Does he get more or less money as a result of school performance? Does he get more or less praise or acceptance from his parents as a result of school performance? The obvious difference between him and his parents is that for him the consequences follow regardless of his performance. This is a point at which mother love may be a liability in child rearing; to give a child his allowance even if he has not done the things he agreed to do, to give a child who performs poorly love and parental attention for nothing in particular, is to provide a situation for a disastrous level of performance.

It is not suggested here that a single bit of mother love or
parental attention be denied but rather that it be used to encour-

## EXPERIMENT 23:

### Contingency Contracting

Contracts usually state what one
person will do for another and what will
be done in return. Contingency refers to
the relationship between events — if A
happens then B will happen. So a contingency contract states that if A does some
specified activity then B will do something
in return.

Robert[33] was careless about his
homework and classwork. He required
constant "pushing" and nagging. His
parents and his teacher cooperated with
Robert in drawing up a contract. To do
this they needed to do three things: specify the key behaviors; identify the present
consequences maintaining the bad situation; and identify the rewards (privileges,
foods, or material things), or punishments
(work, restrictions, etc.) that might control his behavior.

The contract specified which of
Robert's behaviors his parents would
award points for. It also specified what
the points could be used for: homework
completed (three points), well done (five
points), started without warning (five
points), with one warning (three points),
two warnings (two points), three warnings
(one point); on daily grades: A (ten points),
B (six points), C (three points), D (one
point).

The points could be used for the
following according to the contract: outdoor time (five points/half hour), TV
(five points/half hour), cooking (five
points/half hour), driving (ten points/half
hour), going out (ten points), spending the
night with a friend (twenty-five points),
and money (five cents/point).

The contract procedure can be
used to program some rules that encourage progressive behaviors which lead to the
desired performance. Sally was a school
phobic whose contract provided that if
she got out of bed to go to school she received five points, and for other steps
along the way she received more: having
breakfast (five points), no crying before
school (five points), no illness before
school (five points), going to, and getting
on the bus (five points each), arriving at,
going into, and staying in class (five points
each), etc. Again, the points were used to
"buy" privileges at home.

A very important aspect of the contingency contract is to keep a running
record of the performance both in terms
of the child's behavior and in terms of
the pay-offs. A chart on the kitchen wall
would come in handy again here.

age the growth of the child. For the school problem, consequences must be given for the small behaviors that will allow the child to discover that the problem is surmountable. For this purpose you will need a strategy, a plan for what will be done every time the child behaves correctly. This strategy should include planning a situation in which the probability of the correct behavior will be maximized—allowing more frequent support and consequences.

## OBJECTIVES   *chapter seven*

1.   Define modeling.

2.   Why is a gang generally more effective than the parents in shaping behavior? Give two reasons.

3.   Give two reasons why jealousy and fighting over parental rewards occur.

4.   Why is it important that the only child have long periods of contact with other children?

5.   What is rule-testing?

6.   How may complaining be an instance of rule testing? When is complaining not an instance of rule testing?

7.   List seven specific things a parent can do to help the child who is performing poorly in school.

8.   Why is homework behavior difficult to maintain?

9.   How can "learning by doing" be helpful in the homework situation?

10.  Why are children usually unhappy at school?

# 8 / *Attention-Getting Behavior*

**P**arents may suspect that some of their child's bad behavior occurs because of the attention it attracts. Their first step toward seeking a solution should be to ask, "Why can't my child get the attention he needs through other behaviors?" One answer might be that the child does not receive attention or consideration in family activities until he draws attention to himself by being emotional. In other words, he has settled on this solution for getting what he wants because there are no other solutions. A second answer, which is probably more generally the case, is that other solutions do provide some considerations but the overall amount of attention that he receives is small and he receives more attention for bad behaviors than for good ones.

## The Spoiled Child

The spoiled child has found a way to control his parents' behavior. The behavior he uses is usually embarrassing to his parents, and it is emotional. He uses it because it works. If this is the case, you might begin to plan a strategy by making a new effort to define good behaviors that can be rewarded. Another method that might be involved in your strategy is to state an extinction rule for the obnoxious behavior. Single out one aspect of the behavior you are calling spoiled and state a rule about it. For example, if the child begins to cry when he is about to be deprived of something, eliminate the possibility of any change in your decision to deprive him of this particular thing. Notice that the rule singles out crying and does not include getting angry, pouting, or any other aspect of the obnoxious behavior that might be considered part of being spoiled. To attempt to extinguish all spoiled behavior at once is probably impractical, for the rule would be too broad and would force you to look at too many behaviors at one time.

Remember that a spoiled child is spoiled not because of *how much* he gets from his parents but because of *how* he gets it. Many children from poor families are spoiled, and many children from rich families are not.

Perhaps the child receives material possessions from his parents for no particular behavior at all, or perhaps he receives them when he acts especially bad. In the first case, no rule or information about behavior is conveyed to the child by the rewards, so he must cast about in an unstructured environment and come up with his own ideas of what good behavior is. Sometimes he comes up with very poor ideas. In the second case, where rewards are given for bad behavior, a structure and a process are building poor behavior. The second situation is probably more dangerous than the first; at least in the first there is a chance that the child himself will discover acceptable and mature behaviors.

## Crying

Complaining, throwing tantrums, and frequent crying all have something in common: they are directed at the parents and are, at least in part, maintained by attention from the parents. In the case of crying, however, there are some physical aspects of the situation that increase or decrease its frequency. Your kitchen chart can come in handy at this point. Keep a record of when crying occurs and note the reasons for it. You may already suspect that part of the crying is a result of fatigue late in the day or that it is being used on particular persons in the family and occurs only when they are around. These are correctable situations; they may involve changes in the family schedule rather than a manipulation of consequences. Possibly the afternoon nap has been removed too soon or possibly crying always improves the chances that a sibling will be punished. Such supports of crying behavior will of course eventually result in the label "spoiled child."

## Dropping and Throwing

Dropping and throwing are mentioned here because they are similar to a number of other attention-getting behaviors. A child who throws his spoon from his highchair has found a very easy way to get his mother to pay a little bit more attention to him while he eats. Again, the emphasis must be the definition of good behaviors that will receive the attention as well as the extinction of bad behaviors.

## Behavior During Illness

When a child becomes ill, the rules by which he receives attention usually change. Demands that the child do things on his own and take care of himself are reduced. He receives these reductions in demand and increases in reward because he is ill.

If the child learns that he will receive advantages whenever he *says* he is ill, you are in trouble. There will be references to illness that you cannot verify—a headache, an arm ache, or an upset stomach is a hard claim to check out. Even the child may not be able to tell that he is exaggerating and using certain verbal behaviors to control the attention of his parents.

Again, positively stated rules that allow the parent to love and attend the child for good reasons are part of the solution. Also, some of the less attractive but logical consequences of being ill might be emphasized whenever there is reason for suspicion. For example, if the child claims he has a headache, perhaps your first response should be that he lie down and take a nap rather than that he watch television instead of doing homework. Reasonable suggestions should become a consistent and rather prompt reaction on your part to a child who is beginning to use illness for some of its beneficial effects. It is difficult to argue with a child about whether he really has a headache. To prolong the discussion is merely to increase the probability that some reward is being given for improper behavior. If the child says he has a headache, then it is best to act as if it were true but certainly without emphasizing the events that would be beneficial to him.

A child who can always get whatever he wants for dinner, whether it is on the table or not, by claiming that he has a stomach ache will, at times, claim he has a stomach ache. But if this claim constantly results in the limitations and restrictions that would be used for an adult, then faking a stomach ache will be less of a temptation.

### The "Linus" Syndrome

Thumb sucking and overt use of comforters such as blankets, tends to be an attention-getting device. If it is used in this way, the strategy should include the designation of good behaviors that will be attended as well as an extinction procedure for the thumb sucking itself. At times, however, thumb sucking may be considered a compulsive behavior and dealt with as are the other compulsions discussed later in this chapter.

The parent usually states the problem of the comforter in terms of how he can get rid of it. No one seems to mind a one-year-old carrying around his favorite blanket, but as a child reaches his second or third birthday, this behavior can become a problem. First, you might recognize that one hardly ever sees the problem in an eighteen-year-old and that it must disappear somewhere along the way for most children. So although you may believe that you are working against a very emotional, permanent, and perhaps slightly disturbed behavior, take heart in the fact that hardly any children continue this behavior forever. With this in mind, ask yourself if this behavior is really worth the attention it is getting. If it is not damaging to the child at the present time and there is every reason to predict that the child will eventually give it up on his own, isn't your concern primarily selfish? You don't like it because it is embarrassing to you. If after carefully considering these questions you still believe it is time to do something about the comforter, then consider the following alternatives.

If you are considering the immediate and abrupt removal of the comforter, think of Linus' reaction when Snoopy or Lucy snatches his blanket. It is an emotional reaction. It is unreasonable. And it is likely to attract a lot of attention, although it doesn't seem to in the comic strip "Peanuts." Therefore, the danger of immediately taking away the comforter is that obnoxious behaviors are likely to result, and when they do they may be rewarded with frantic attention.

The second alternative for the removal of the comforter is to present some enforceable fading technique. You might start by limiting *when* the comforter will be available. You might say that from the time the child gets up in the morning until 7:30 A.M. he may not have the comforter, but after that he may. You might establish the time as 8:00 A.M. in the second week, then increase the interval daily, but always beginning with the early part of the day, when he is rested.

Another way to use a fading technique is to limit *where* the comforter will be available. This technique is similar to reducing smoking in adults by designating a "smoking chair." The procedure utilizes a chair in the household that is considered the only place in which the undesirable item can be used. Furthermore, when the subject is in this chair, he can do nothing but have the undesirable item. No conversation. No reading. No watching TV. For example, you might designate a chair in the living room as the only place in which the comforter is available. The problem with this technique is that you must plan what consequence will occur if the child refuses to play the rules of the game. If he gets out of the chair and takes the comforter with him, what will you do? You take away the undesirable item. In a way, the procedure rewards the child for sitting in a chair by allowing him the comforter there. At first, he may sit in the chair quite a bit, but he will tire of that. As you can see, this last solution becomes a rather time-consuming one compared with the size of the problem.

## Tantrums

A tantrum is one of the most obvious examples of a bad behavior that is maintained by rewards, and the most obvious reward is the object being demanded by the child. If he gets his way (and his toy) by throwing a tantrum, then he is likely to throw a tantrum the next time he wants his way. A more subtle source of reward for the tantrum is the attention that the parents give. The attention includes not only consoling but reprimanding that might be done to stop the child's tantrum.

---

## EXPERIMENT 24

### Turning the Reward Away From Thumbsucking

Audrey, Betty, and Carol[34] were all third graders with a thumbsucking problem. Audrey was uncomfortable in class, always vying for teacher attention, and blaming herself for failures. Betty was moody and insolent, and sucked her thumb whenever scolded. Carol was a better student but thumbsucked when she was tired or bored.

A special teacher had the girls two days a week in class, and brought observers in to measure the amount of time each girl spent thumbsucking. After four days of observation, the teacher began praising the girls for other behaviors which were difficult or impossible to do while thumbsucking. These "incompatible" behaviors were: folding hands on the desk, folding arms on the desk, and writing in a notebook.

Of course, the teacher couldn't possibly "catch the girls being good" every time, and praise or encourage them in every instance. She had over 30 students in the class. Nevertheless, for the next four days she did her best to reward these good behaviors often. Then she stopped rewarding them for four days, and then started rewards again for another four days. Figure 18 shows how thumbsucking went down when other behaviors were rewarded.

**FIGURE 18**

Duration of Betty's poor behavior when reinforcement was used. (Audrey and Carol showed similar results.)

(Adapted with permission of the **Journal of Applied Behavior Analysis.** Skiba, E.A., Pettigrew, E. and Alden, S.E. "A behavioral approach to the control of thumbsucking in the classroom." **Journal of Applied Behavior Analysis.** 1971, 4, 123. Copyright 1971 by the Society for the Experimental Analysis of Behavior, Inc.)

When a request is made by a child who occasionally throws tantrums, the parent should make a careful decision. If his decision is to deny the request, then the tantrum should not be allowed to alter that decision. To respond to such a child by saying, "I'll think about it," or "We'll have to wait until your father comes home," is to set up a situation in which the child is very likely to give you the tantrum. In a way, delaying the decision is at least a temporary denial of the request, but it is done in a weak way and therefore tempts the child to fight for what he wants. Because the child occasionally throws tantrums as a reaction to a denial, you may find that he throws tantrums as a reaction to merely being put off for a while. Emotionality is a common reaction to problems for which there seem to be no solutions. By putting off a child for a few hours, by denying him an answer, you have set up a situation in which there is no solution for a long period of time—plenty of time to try out a tantrum. So your refusal to give a straightforward answer may further complicate the tantrum problem.

Another complication in putting off a child who occasionally throws tantrums is that the lack of a decision may leave the child with nothing specific to do. It is difficult for a child to set aside one line of activity and switch to some other activity for a time because a decision has not yet come down from the powers that be. He continues to complain and nag because he has nothing else to do and because he is trying to speed up the decision. The lack of something to do is a frustration, and the complaining and nagging can quickly build up to a tantrum.

Once you have answered your child's question or request or put him off until some later time, he is not likely to attract your attention unless he performs in some loud and clear way. In Chapter 5 tantrums were used as an example of the reward value of attention. It was also pointed out how tantrums might be developed from simple crying and complaining. If the parents decide to allow the child to cry it out but merely wait until the crying has been loud and long, then of course they are demanding a louder and longer behavior for their attention and the child is likely to learn it.

## Fears

One of the major difficulties in dealing with unreasonable fears in children is that adults forget that fears are also behaviors. They are a result of experience, they are followed by consequences, and they are observed in others. Usually fears result from a combination of factors, and some of these should receive special attention.

In most cases, childhood fears are learned from parents. Whenever a child has an unreasonable fear, his parents usually have the same fear to some unreasonable degree. So the first question to ask is "Did he learn the fear from me, and do I continue to be his example?"

A second question to ask is the now familiar "What happens

---

## EXPERIMENT 25

### Negative Practice

Ted[35] averaged 140 obscenities per hour in the classroom. If you had tape-recorded him and then deleted the expletives you would have had a lot of silent tape! At the age of ten he seemed to have developed a very repetitive use of bad words. He repeated them reflexively, out of context, in a stuttering sort of way.

After four days of baseline (a rather peculiar experience for the observer) the teacher took Ted into a small room adjacent to the classroom for a 15-minute period and instructed him to repeat rapidly the most frequent obscene word of the day. If he stopped before the 15-minute period ended, the teacher urged him to continue. This "forced negative practice" reduced his classroom rate of swearing to about 90 per hour in eight days.

Then the small room was used as a time out room. With each occurrence of obscene language, Ted was taken to this bare room for five minutes or until he maintained one minute of silence, whichever occurred first. His swearing rate dropped to ten per hour and finally to less than five.

next?" Does he get to sleep with you when he is afraid of the dark? Do you sit with him in his room when he is afraid of being alone? Do you carry him when dogs are around? All these reactions are acceptable ways of helping a child through a difficult moment, but if they become habits, the love that motivated them builds bad behavior.

A third question concerns consequences too, but here the behavior may be one other than the fear. Is the child afraid of being alone because in the past he has been punished for other bad behaviors by being put in a room alone? Consider the fear of being put to bed and left alone. Perhaps the child has been punished repeatedly in this situation for failing to go to sleep or making noise at night or for bed wetting or masturbating. These punishments cannot be taken back, but they can give you a better understanding of your child's present fears and help you avoid some in the future.

As we have emphasized, the first question to ask in a strategy session is whether or not the problem is serious enough to require attention. If you decide that it is not, then your reactions should be watched to see that you and your spouse do not give any serious reactions to the future occurrences of the emotional behavior.

When a specific fear is the problem, another question might be whether the object or situation that is feared can be easily avoided. If the child is afraid of the dark, is there something wrong with leaving a light on? The opposite strategy—forcing the feared object or situation upon the child—is usually not effective. Dragging a kicking and screaming child up to a dog in order to "get him to understand" that most dogs are nice only makes him fear you as well as the dogs.

Most childhood fears fade away naturally as a result of varying degrees of exposure to the feared object. The parent should keep in mind, however, that the emotional behavior fades away only if there is no attention-getting aspect of the consequences for the fear to maintain it.

## Compulsions

Compulsions such as nail biting, hair twirling, nose picking, and lip biting are usually maintained partly by parental attention and partly by the absence of something else to do. They are behaviors that fill up time and are occasionally rewarded by parents. Like stuttering, such behaviors seem to be magnified by social pressures and hurried situations. Tense situations in which the child has nothing to do provide the greatest opportunity for compulsive behavior. If a little supportive attention from the parents is also present, a compulsion can become a serious problem.

If you believe the compulsion deserves concern, then you might try one of the following strategies. The first and most

---

## EXPERIMENT 26

### Modification Techniques with Fear and Depression

Mrs. W[36], age fifty-one, had a fear of being closed in. Her claustrophobic reactions occurred when she was closed in a house by herself, in a car alone, in church, at the movies, etc. Even when she went to a ladies' room, her son had to stand outside and hold the door slightly ajar so that someone was "near" and she was not "closed in".

Although she had made progress with a therapist (the two gradually worked up to a nine-minute period in a small room), the therapist had to remain just outside the room when she was alone. If he were to go down the hall to another room, Mrs. W had to leave the small room in about four minutes.

The experimenter then provided a stopwatch. He explained its operation, and asked Mrs. W to monitor her time so that an electric timer could be checked against it for accuracy. With this new source of information about her own success right in front of her, she progressed to remaining alone in the room for almost six minutes.

Then the stopwatch was removed and Mrs. W tried going it alone. She could still remain for five or six minutes but there was no more improvement. When the stopwatch was returned, she began improving again. Just feedback about the behavior was helpful.

appropriate approach is to consider the situations in which the compulsion occurs and determine if anything about your reactions to your child's behavior could alleviate some of the tension in such environments. Another strategy frequently used is to reward the lack of compulsive behavior. For example, a mother promised a dollar to her son if he could refrain from nail biting long enough for his nails to require cutting. Because this demand of behavior seemed a bit too large for a first step, the child was also given a nickle for each one of his fingernails that needed trimming because it had been allowed to grow.

Such a direct contingency upon a compulsive behavior must be used carefully. There is always a tendency to do more than state the rule, and nagging ensures that some verbal attention will be connected with errors. As is the case for any of the

Miss V[37], age twenty, had been hospitalized for six years because of "anxiety-depression.". She often cried and for no reason, felt that everyone hated her, was withdrawn and fearful. She often expressed her fear about possible injury and death.

In that hospital patients could earn tokens for various jobs and good behaviors. These were used to buy privileges: TV, field trips, and so forth. Aides on Miss V's ward recorded her crying and smiling behavior, and after two weeks began using the tokens to reward smiling. They also removed tokens for crying. Miss V now had to pay for the privilege of crying.

Over the next six weeks crying went almost to zero and smiling increased (see "tokens" in Figures 19 and 20). When the procedure was stopped things got worse again ("extinction" in each of the graphs). When crying was rewarded things became almost as bad as they were before the procedure was started.

The aides then began praising and encouraging Miss V's smiling. They also resumed giving her tokens for smiling. Then slowly the tokens were faded out and smiling was maintained by social rewards alone. Miss V was not "cured" but, due to rewards for good behavior, she was finally showing improvement after six years of hospitalization.

strategies above, social attention for the compulsion should be avoided.

Remember that if a child has elected to work for attention, then—at least in the child's view—he is not getting enough attention. If attention for the compulsion is removed, attention will have to be added for some more pleasant behavior.

## Stuttering

Stuttering is at least partially related to the social pressures of a situation and usually occurs more frequently when the subject is

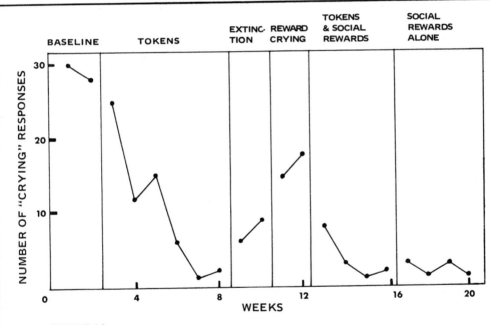

**FIGURE 19**
Total crying responses during the weeks of different token reinforcement.

(Adapted with permission of the **Journal of Applied Behavior Analysis.** Reisinger, J.J. "The treatment of 'anxiety-depression' via positive reinforcement and response cost." **Journal of Applied Behavior Analysis.** 1972, 5, 129. Copyright 1972 by the Society for the Experimental Analysis of Behavior, Inc.)

in an argument, in an intense social situation, or in a hurry to communicate to someone. Thus, although there are many aspects of the stuttering problem that require professional attention, the people around the stutterer provide some of the reasons for the stuttering.

The situation can be partly eased by providing enough family time to allow good behavior to occur. It is easy to become impatient with a child who has not yet acquired the verbal facility for talking at the rate of speed demanded by adults. If you continue to allow the minimum amount of time for good

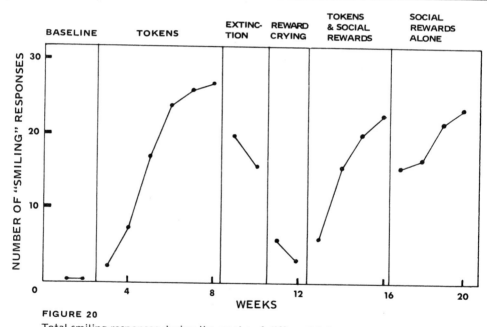

**FIGURE 20**

Total smiling responses during the weeks of different token reinforcement.

(Adapted with permission of the **Journal of Applied Behavior Analysis.** Reisinger, J.J. "The treatment of 'anxiety-depression' via positive reinforcement and response cost." **Journal of Applied Behavior Analysis.** 1972, 5, 129. Copyright 1972 by the Society for the Experimental Analysis of Behavior, Inc.)

behaviors to occur, then you probably find little opportunity to reward good behaviors. To complete sentences for a child who is hesitating or to supply vocabulary to a child who cannot at the moment seem to find the right word is the surest way to communicate your impatience. Learn to give the stutterer time.

For the occasional stutterer there may be even more specific situations than those described above. For example, many people do not stutter at all when dealing with their own family but develop their difficulties only in public situations. If this is the case for your child, your family can help by providing an atmosphere similar to the one described above when the child is in public situations.

## Rhythmic Habits

Such habits as tapping a pencil, swinging the foot, and rocking to the rhythm of music are common pastimes of children. If these are annoyances, they seem too trivial to bother with. They are the common behaviors of healthy, energetic children. At their extremes however, these behaviors can rise to such a frequency that they compete with more productive behaviors and may be physically damaging to the child. Usually the term "compulsion" is applied to such a behavior.

Most mothers of children with such habits can remember the beginning of the behavior as less frequent and noncompulsive. Usually an overly concerned parent designated the rhythmic habit as a problem before it actually became one. As a matter of fact, it may be *because* she designated the habit a problem that it became a problem. This change may occur because as soon as the behavior is labeled a problem, the parents begin to give it a lot of attention. It becomes a gimmick by which the child can get through to the parents. Getting through to the parents may bring about a punitive kind of attention or some more positive reaction, but in either case the rhythmic habit is strengthened over other possible behaviors.

So again the rhythmic habit falls under the category of an attention-getting activity, and again the extinction procedure for such an activity will have to be accompanied by a designated good behavior to be rewarded by the attention.

## Toilet Training

Most psychologists consider toilet training to be one of the crucial areas of child rearing because most people seem to consider it such an emotional time. If you consider the behaviors that occur during toilet training, however, you find that the emotional behaviors are those of the parents rather than those of the child. The fact that the parents consider toilet training a crucial area makes it crucial.

If there is emotionality on the part of the child, it may come from the punishment given by the parents for "mistakes." Punishment is usually accompanied by a great deal of emotion, which makes the situation very disruptive for the parents and for the child. Thus, it would be best to maximize the possibilities of giving rewards for successful behaviors and to minimize the chances of making mistakes and punishing a child emotionally for his mistakes.

First, you need some way of knowing when successes are likely to occur. As was noted in Chapter 2, the best way of determining timing is to place a chart above the diaper pail in the bathroom and hang a pencil next to this chart so that you can make marks on it conveniently. Across the top, list the hours of the day from the time the child gets up until well after he has gone to bed. Label rows on the chart for days. If you use a check for urination and a cross for defecation whenever you place a diaper in the diaper pail, you can begin to get some notion of when each of these events occurs during the day. After many days of filling out the chart, you can look at the columns and see at what time it would be best to put the child on the toilet. Now at least you will not put him on the toilet at times when you know he will fail, and you will not have to sit around with him for long, frustrating periods.

When you start learning, don't stop the chart. Continue to collect your information on the chart and also add another kind of mark that can tell you when the child is successful.

What consequence will you use for successes? When your child is this young—two and a half or three—it is best to use a concrete reward to motivate him to learn. Therefore, it is seriously suggested that you place a special jar of candies (M&Ms, for example) in the bathroom so that it can be given out in very small portions. For each small success, give the child a candy—or even put it right into his mouth, for the immediacy of the reward is extremely important. But what level of behavior should be asked for for those first rewards? Again, you must be sure that your demands are easy enough to ensure that some reward will be given even on the first day, although you know that a successful visit to the toilet is not probable then. So you might begin by merely rewarding the child for sitting on the pot.

Some children have been exposed so long to an emotional toilet-training experience that they will not go near the toilet or possibly even the bathroom. In such cases the fading procedure will have to begin in some other situation than it would ordinarily. For example, you might begin by giving the child a small piece of candy for sitting on a portable pot in his room, then in the hall, then in the bathroom, and finally on top of the regular toilet. Remember that a fading procedure is an honest one and that the changes in the rules should be stated in advance—for example, "Tomorrow I'm going to move the potty into the bathroom, and you can sit on it in there to get your candies." State this change in the rules at the time you are giving the last reward for sitting on the pot in the child's room. Don't suddenly change the rules. Warn him. And warn him at a good time—that is, when other rewards are still being given.

There are probably two kinds of accidents from the parents'

## EXPERIMENT 27

### Paying for Paying Attention

At age five and a half, David[38] gave his parents a very hard time. He averaged one full-blown tantrum each day — sometimes many more. He screamed, kicked, threw things, and occasionally hit his sister or parents. Talking, spanking, reasoning, and sending David to his room had all been tried. In addition to his tantrum behavior, David also wet the bed four or five times each week.

Most of these behaviors occurred when David's parents asked him to do something (such as go to bed, complete his chores, etc.). So the behavior was called oppositional. Observers started counting these oppositional behaviors for the half-hour preceding bedtime. Every 20 seconds they recorded whether or not any oppositional behavior (i.e., failure to obey parents' request within 20 seconds, including yelling, screaming, or hitting) had occurred, and whether or not any cooperative behavior had occurred.

During this baseline period it would be possible for David to score 90 points for oppositional behavior in ninety 20-second intervals in the 30-minute period if he was absolutely terrible. Of course, he could also get 90 marks for cooperative behavior. For each 20-second period in which David continued to be cooperative (or oppositional) he was scored in the

appropriate category even when no more requests were made.

Ordinarily, the parents ignored David's behavior when he wasn't giving them trouble. But when he hit his sister, or started a tantrum they immediately paid attention to him. After three weeks the parents were asked to change their habits. They were asked to ignore the bad behaviors as much as possible (short of damage to David's sister), and to watch for cooperative behavior which they were to reward with hugs, and praise, such as "Good boy, David", or "David, we're proud of you when you behave like that."

In addition, a corner of David's room was used as a time-out place. David was placed there when he was bad, and left there until ten minutes had passed or his tantrum had been over for several minutes. At bedtime he was to be put to bed and his parents were to ignore his screaming and crying.

The graph in Figure 21 shows that during baseline David was oppositional about 25% to 33% of the time, and cooperative about 10% of the time. He also wet the bed on an average of two times a week. When the new procedure was used for two weeks, oppositional behavior dropped to less than 10%. Cooperative behavior took over 50% of the time. There was only one case of bed wetting. The experimenter then asked his mother and father to return to their old habits (baseline two). The results were seven bed wettings in two weeks and bad ole' David during the day. After that, the new procedure was used continuously, and the righthand part of the graph shows the good results.

The experimenter checked occasionally over the next year and a half. He found the improved situation continued and there was no bed wetting in sixteen months! Here is a case where a new strategy dealing with poor behaviors had the additional benefit of alleviating an "emotional" problem, for no particular consequence was given to bed wetting but it improved anyway.

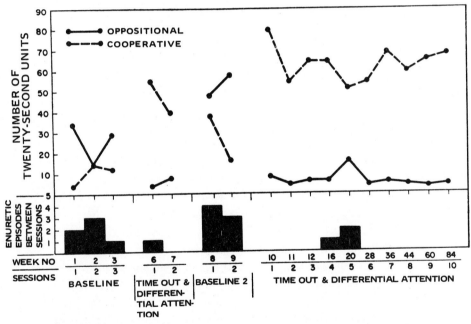

**FIGURE 21**

David's oppositional, cooperative, and bed wetting behavior during experimental conditions.

(Reprinted with permission of the **Journal of Applied Behavior Analysis.** Nordquist, V.M. "The modification of a child's enuresis: Some response-response relationships." **Journal of Applied Behavior Analysis.** 1971, 4, 244. Copyright 1971 by the Society for the Experimental Analysis of Behavior, Inc.)

point of view. The first is one in which the child "warns" the mother too late to get the child to the bathroom. In this case the child has performed part of the behavior you wanted and should be rewarded, at first, for having given such a warning. The reward should be concrete as well as social. The other kind of accident is discovered by the parent only after it has occurred; there has been no warning by the child. The use of punishment would seem to be called for in this case. But punishment is useful only when it is used in an immediate and consistent way, and because of the manner in which this behavior is discovered, it is usually too late to use any consequence. Therefore, no punishment for discovered accidents is advised. The child should be told that he has made a mistake, but he should not be punished, reprimanded, or yelled at as punishment.

### Bed Wetting

Often, bed wetting is a medical problem, for certain infections of the bladder and urinary tract can produce uncontrolled urination. Therefore, one of the first tests for this behavioral problem should be a urine analysis by your physician. When you are sure that there are no physical ailments involved in the child's bed wetting, you might consult the Sears catalog for a harmless device that is very effective in controlling bed wetting. Two pads of metal foil with a fiberglass lining between them are placed under the bed sheets and are not in the least uncomfortable to the child. As soon as urination begins, the dampness in the fiberglass lining activates a buzzer, which sounds similar to an alarm clock. Because bed wetting begins intermittently, there is still time for the child to wake up and go to the bathroom as he should. Over a period of days this device teaches the child to control urination and to wake up and use the bathroom. This "alarm clock for bed wetting" has been found to be extremely effective for normal children not afflicted with diseases of the urinary tract.

Bed wetting should not be considered as just a basic emotional problem. Categorizing bed wetting as an emotional problem is an excuse for not doing anything to help the child. Many parents note that bed wetting is related to how good a day the child had or to whether the child was at home in his own bed or not. So the bed wetting behavior is not as "uncontrollable" as the child (and some adults) would have you believe.

In addition to using the alarm clock for bed wetting, the simple consequence of having the child take care of (change and remake) his own bed has been successful. Some parents have also had their child do whatever part he can to help wash his own sheets. This strategy is logical and straightforward, and it is a good education for the child. Furthermore, it addresses itself directly to the child who is supposedly "just too lazy to get up" during the night. If laziness is a problem, then the price of laziness will have to be raised. Hopefully, this price can be raised in a logical, almost nonpunitive way.

## OBJECTIVES    *chapter eight*

1.  What are two reasons for "why can't my child get the attention he needs through other (than bad) behaviors?"

2.  What are two methods for dealing with a child's bad behavior?

3.  Why is it impractical to attempt to extinguish all spoiled behaviors at once?

4.  What are the two possible outcomes of rewarding a child for no particular behavior at all?

5.  What is the likely consequence of abruptly snatching away a child's comforter?

6.  What are two alternatives for removal of the child's comforter?

7.  Give two reasons why delaying a decision on a child's request can lead to a tantrum.

8.  What are two possible strategies to deal with compulsive behavior?

9.  When does stuttering frequently occur? What are two good ways to communicate your impatience with the child's verbal behavior?

10. How can designating a behavior as a problem result in it actually becoming one?

11. Why is toilet training considered a crucial area of child rearing? How could a chart be useful in toilet training?

12. Describe the fading procedure for overcoming the child's aversion to the toilet.

13. What are the two kinds of accidents from the parent's point of view?

14. What is the first thing that should be done if the child has a bedwetting problem?

# 9 / Expanding Areas of Responsibility

**W**hen a child learns to do chores and develop everyday living habits, there is a double benefit. The child learns something about the management of his own life and the parents benefit by reducing their work load a little. Because of this double benefit, some parents have mixed feelings about requiring the chores to be done. Parents sometimes feel that rewards for chores should be unnecessary, yet at the same time they feel some guilt because of the personal benefit they derive.

Parents should understand, however, that the management of daily chores requires a reward plan just as any other behavior does. Moreover, parents should feel no guilt about personal benefits, because it's better that the child be gradually trained with rewards than to have the total drudgery thrust upon him later.

## Room Cleaning

The child's habit of keeping his room in order begins the first time his parents ask him to pick up his toys. When this request is made and the behavior is given, the parents have their first opportunity to provide consequences for this correct behavior and thereby shape the probability that it will occur in the future.

Start right here. You've asked for some small part of room cleaning so reward it. Building small habits early is better than letting the child become dependent and then deciding, "it's time you did your own cleaning." If it is time, then parts of the total job should have been shaped up in advance—otherwise it isn't time. The social rewards are, of course, those ordinarily used in these circumstances, and they can be very effective. But sometimes a concrete reward is necessary to get the complete job done. Unfortunately, parents usually want to give this reward only when the whole job is done, which leads to the problem of defining the finished job.

The most effective way to plan the reward of some general duty of the child is to prepare a check list that spells out in detail the little things that must be done to add up to a finished job. For room cleaning, the check list might include "bedspread straight; toys off the floor; lamps, chairs, and desk items in the proper place; floor vacuumed or swept; and clothes hung in the proper place." If this check list is posted in the child's room so that he can see what items are yet to be done, then you can avoid nagging him and chipping away at his resistance to do each of the small jobs and a straightforward rule about consequences can be formed. The rule might be that when the check list is completed, some of the child's allowance will be given to him. Check lists should be approved at a certain time of the day. The room-cleaning rule should include a deadline, so that there is no opportunity for procrastinating on the child's part or nagging on the parents' part. If the check list items are not completed by a certain time, the positive consequence will not occur.

The parents may find themselves continually agitated if they draw up too detailed a description of the various habits of neatness of their child. Draw up the chart with your child's help. Use liberal definitions of what a good job is. Don't impose your idea of perfection where her idea of "good enough" will do. Don't lose sight of what you want—a reasonably presentable room will do. It's her room and she probably lives in it more than you live in yours. So accept definitions of "good enough" which are short of the neatness of a department store window.

The major point to remember in all this negotiation is whose privacy—whose territory—we're talking about. The one who has to live with it should have the most say. The parent has the responsibility of teaching the minimum standards.

This notion of individuality is also important when selecting furniture and decorations. Give the child a say here too. How can he get interested in cleaning up his room if all the furniture in it is selected by his parents, arranged by his parents, cleaned by his parents, and approved by his parents? The organization and decoration of the room might be best left to the child, so that he can have some personal interest in the project. If he feels that he is merely performing duties that you should perform because you are the one who takes most of the responsibility, you may find the job of teaching him to care for his room an uphill battle.

## Dressing

In dressing, as in caring for a room, the margin for individuality is important. It is difficult to become vitally interested in a project that is someone else's idea and someone else's responsibility. If you select all the clothes for your child, buy them, wash them, and iron them, do not be surprised if he does not seem too interested in what he wears or how he looks.

One of the best ways of controlling the way a child dresses is to use matching funds. The rule is that every dollar the child is willing to spend on his clothes is matched by another dollar from his parents. When the child buys clothes, he uses his own money but because of the matching fund he has a substantial amount with which to buy something worthwhile. If he is also allowed to participate to a great extent in the decision making that accompanies the shopping, his interest in the way he looks may increase.

Although the matching-fund notion usually increases the interest and responsibility that the child feels concerning his own clothes, there may be an additional problem if he does not take care of them. Clothes care can be included on the same check list used for room cleaning and thereby brought under the control of some positive consequence. Between the two notions of positive consequence and the opportunity to feel responsible, most of the neatness problem can be avoided.

## Sleep

Sleep problems can be influenced by exercise and deprivation of the child during the day. So the first point is not to approach the problem as if it could be influenced by consequences but rather to approach the problem as if it could be influenced by the behaviors of the child that occur during the day. Is the child ready to sleep? This is a condition over which parents can exert some control, but usually do not. The amount of exercise a child gets during the day can be influenced by the rules concerning his play. The amount of his sleep deprivation can be influenced by the rigidity or liberalness of the rules concerning nap time. Sometimes parents think they are somewhat in the hands of fate with regard to how their child feels at bedtime, but actually they are the primary influence on how he feels.

Many of the behaviors connected with bedtime are of an attention-getting variety. Whimpering, head banging, and calling for water or lights are all behaviors that should be regarded with suspicion by parents. Often these behaviors have been developed by the parents, who prolong the child's bedtime activity themselves. At this last event of the day, many parents suddenly feel that they have not given the child enough time, and they tarry with him. If you feel this way, you should at least keep your child out of bed during this pleasant interval and talk with him or play with him elsewhere in his room or in the house.

There should be one signal that reliably indicates that it is bedtime and that the child should go to sleep. This signal is the process of putting him into the bed and tucking him in. This is not to say that bedtime lullabies, rocking, and patting are necessarily bad. But parents should carefully observe *why* they engage in these behaviors. If these behaviors are more likely to be given to the child when he whines or protests, then the parents are building something that they may not like.

Be careful of being too rigid about the time at which a child goes to bed or it will become a rule just asking to be broken. If you select a given time for the child to go to bed, provide some realistic allowance or margin around that time. Within a few years this will be his decision, so start decreasing your control early by widening that margin. Also, his bedtime should not be a direct response to his behavior, such as using an early bedtime to punish his bad behavior. It should be a general decision made by yourself considering what has to be done, how fatigued he is, and what time he has to get up the next day. To use bedtime as a punishment for incorrect behavior only reinforces the child's view that bed is a bad place to go.

A child may refuse to go to sleep for many different reasons. He may not be tired or he may receive a great deal of attention for procrastinating about getting ready for bed or going to sleep, or there may be consequences that occur in the morning *after* his night in bed. For example, one mother complained that her child would "lie in bed half the night" without sleeping. She said that he did not call out or make unnecessary demands while in bed; he would merely lie there without sleeping. When she went to his room to see how he was during the night, she often discovered him wide awake. As it turned out, he had been given many special considerations as a result of losing sleep. His mother had asked his father not to be "too hard on him." She had also written a letter to the child's teacher explaining some of his poor behavior as a result of his lack of sleep. The mother also remembered that she often reprimanded her other children for giving the boy a hard time when he was so tired. She began to realize that she was providing him with a strong reason for continuing to lose sleep. She provided extra protection for him as long as he lacked the proper amount of sleep.

Other instances of childhood insomnia have been shown to be related to consequences that the parents provide. For example, a child who has been severely punished for wet dreams or masturbation during sleep often actively avoids bedtime and sleep. This situation is probably related to the fact that when the child goes to bed, he puts himself in a situation in which he may be tempted to do something which is punished.

It will be necessary to refrain from using punishment on such behaviors as those described above in order to produce better sleeping behavior. The procedure requires a great deal of patience on the part of the parents, however. In the long run, of course, the goal is to allow the child to determine his sleeping habits, and therefore the goal is to remove all consequences for sleeping behaviors.

## Meals

Table manners and social behaviors often go together. A child who eats in a messy way at the table usually disrupts the meal by yelling and carrying on as well. When such a dominating social blunderer is at the dinner table, the parents are likely to pay a great deal of attention to him with reprimands, punishments, and other threats designed to suppress his bad behavior. Selective attention for bad behavior, however, helps perpetuate a mealtime battle that is amusing to the children and disgusting to the parents.

The deterioration of the mealtime atmosphere by bad behavior and punishment seems particularly effective in making the members of the family feel that the whole family situation is miserable. Asking the following three questions may shed light on mealtime problems.

*Are the people who are acting up at dinner hungry when they come to the table?*  The question may suggest that there are times, either before or after dinner, when the parents could withhold food so that the presentation of food at dinnertime would be more important.

*What behaviors of the children should be attended at mealtime?*  This question should be answered with regard to what good behaviors should be attended as well as what bad behaviors are of concern. Further thought will be necessary to decide whether the bad behavior should be attended verbally at the table or whether the show-off should be ignored.

*What is the social context of the mealtime situation?*  To examine this question from the child's point of view, is there any conversation that is of genuine interest to him? If all the conversation is over his head, then the likelihood of his acting up to get attention is greater because (1) he has no other way to draw attention to himself in this adult conversation and (2) the conversation has excluded him so that there really isn't anything else to do anyway.

If the behavior is bad enough that you decide to use some punishment as a means of controlling it, then be careful not to use too many verbal threats about that rule at the dinner table. When verbal threats are prolonged, they become the kind of selective attention for bad behavior discussed above. If you are going to remove a child from the table and have him eat alone in the kitchen whenever he throws his food, then state the rule simply and in the same words each time as soon as he first begins to act up. If his bad behavior continues, carry through on the rule without ceremony. If you think you need ceremony (acting angry, handling him roughly, and so on), then you must believe that removing him is not a good consequence.

## Money

The greatest misers and materialists are children. These little keepers of piggy banks who count and recount the pennies that dribble down from their parents make King Midas look like a philanthropist. Babies don't seem to come into the world with a love for money, so the behaviors connected with money must be learned.

It is not a child's healthy respect for the value and power of money that frightens most parents. Rather, it is the devious ways by which some children attempt to get money. These devious ways may have developed because money is the only reward that the parents have explicitly given as a reward. Possibly this is the only incentive that the parents have ever used consistently. Bring in other rewards (privileges, TV time, your explicit attention and praise).

There is really no problem in using any rules about money except that they are usually of a one-shot nature or at least are applied inconsistently. At one time or another all parents have gone through the process of naming certain tasks that the child could do to "earn his allowance" only to have the demand for the task deteriorate over the weeks while the allowance continues to be given. So usually if a child ends up with a problem about money, it is because he is given too much of it or because he is given too much of it free. Money is a commodity that he will eventually have to work for, and there is no advantage to him to have a time in his life when he doesn't have to work for it.

Using a graduated allowance (see Chapter 10) allows you to apply rules about monetary rewards that can effectively maintain behaviors. This system may give away a great deal of allowance when a child performs well all week, but the fact that he is gaining a great deal of money each week should not be alarming. It is an opportunity to expand his areas of responsibility in controlling some of the activities of his own life. It does not necessarily follow that he has his money merely to spend on whatever he pleases. The areas in which he must pay his own way can be expanded as his improved behavior gains him more payoff from you in the graduated-allowance system. In the long run, it is not necessary for a higher allowance to be more expensive for the parents.

A child who receives an unusually large amount of money for his allowance could be asked to buy some of his clothes, pay for his lunches, pay for his amusements, and therefore learn something about the expense of these day-to-day activities rather than have this opportunity wasted by being told that his allowance is only for special things. Thus, even small children might gain as much as $2, $3, or $5 a week from a graduated-allowance system, but their responsibilities for how the money can be spent could also be expanded. The tremendous advantages of such a parental attitude are that a great deal of behavior is maintained by the graduated allowance and that the child takes over and experiences firsthand some of the more subtle expenses that must be paid.

## Procrastination

Procrastination raises the suspicion of problems with two kinds of consequences. First, the procrastination may be some kind of attention-getting behavior—that is, a reward may occur for not performing the task. Second, the procrastination may occur because the task itself is not rewarded.

The most usual circumstance in which a parent finds his child procrastinating is where a punishment is the consequence. The punishment is threatened by the parent whenever the child says something about putting off the task. This threat acts as selective attention for the procrastinating behavior. Further incentive for the procrastination is that the task itself is done merely to avoid the threatened punishment. There's no positive reason to perform, and completion of the task would terminate the opportunity to procrastinate for verbal attention.

A parent might also suspect that the procrastination has an even more direct positive consequence: the procrastination may eventually be rewarded by the performance of the task *by the parent*. Thus, the procrastination problem may resemble the guff-control situation mentioned in Chapter 2. The main point to understand is that procrastination is not the *lack* of a behavior but is, in itself, a behavior with a consequence.

## Public Behavior

There are two reasons that public behavior exhibited by a child is sometimes different from his behavior at home. The first and most obvious of these is that the rules that are enforced by the parents at home are not enforced in public. These rules may even be replaced by another set of stricter rules that are less consist-

## EXPERIMENT 28

### Weeding Out Some Procrastination

Mrs. J's[39] fifth-grade class included a group of children who always returned late from recess and lunch. They straggled in, disrupting the first part of the class, and requiring instructions to be repeated. Mrs. J was driven to exasperation.

After studying some patriotic books on American history, she announced that the children could be good patriots by being good students (i.e., prompt students). A chart entitled "Today's Patriots" was hung and the names of those students that came in on time after lunch were recorded. Prior to that a record of tardiness had been kept on morning, afternoon, and lunch recesses for 13 days (baseline). The patriot chart was effective in reducing the number of students late after lunch

but left recess tardiness unchanged. After seven days, returning from morning recess was also recorded on the chart. And, six days later the performance after the afternoon recess was added. The graph in Figure 22 shows how decreases in tardiness occurred only when the consequence was made contingent on that particular time of day.

Later the chart was removed, added again, and changed to list only offenders. While the chart listing "Today's Un-Patriots" was used the rule was changed so that an increasing number of days without being late were necessary to remain off the list. After the students were consistently on time for class, using the chart only occasionally was good enough to maintain their behavior.

**FIGURE 22**
Number of tardy pupils related to sessions of using the charts.

(Adapted with permission of the **Journal of Applied Behavior Analysis.** Hall, R.V., Custler, C., Craston, J.S., and Toucker, B. "Teachers and parents as researchers using multiple baseline designs." **Journal of Applied Behavior Analysis.** 1970, 3, 249. Copyright 1971 by the Society for the Experimental Analysis of Behavior, Inc.)

ently enforced. The second reason is that additional rewards are sometimes available from people in public. If a mother who is easily embarrassed refrained from enforcing a given set of rules as long as she was being observed by a stranger, her child would eventually learn to respond differently when other people were watching.

A complicating factor in the public-behavior problem occurs when the rules have been changed so that they are more severe. Most of the rules that change when a parent enters a public place with her child are concerned with consequences involving punishment. Such consequences attract increased attention from strangers and therefore put the child "on stage" even more. His stage performance in these cases will dramatize any emotion that he might be able to create. For example, he may try playing Cute Little Devil or Mistreated Prisoner or, as a last resort, Justified Fury. In each case one eye is upon the usual source of consequences (the parents) but the other eye is upon the strangers who are present. A child's change in behavior rests entirely upon the notion that his parents are watching these strangers and are being influenced by their reactions also.

It is probably important to point out that the public situation should cause no particular change in the rules agreed upon by the parents. No amount of emotional behavior on the part of the child should bring about any unique reaction on the part of the parent. If a unique reaction does occur, this is the stuff tantrums are made of. When a child does intend to embarrass his mother through extreme emotional behavior, the best recourse is probably to remove him from the public situation immediately. This may mean that she has to interrupt her shopping trip and it may mean that she and the child both must go home at once. But the child should not be allowed to get away with extreme emotional behavior just because he is a child. In these difficult situations it is probably most useful to ask what your reaction would be if the problem person were an adult rather than a child. The answer to this question sometimes produces the most reasonable and straightforward means of dealing with the problem. You would leave, taking him or her with you if you had to; but you certainly wouldn't stay and endure the embarrassment of a public scene.

## Sex Education

The trend in sex education, as everyone knows, is to tell all when the child is very young. The trend may be a healthy development, but the important point is how this education influences present and future sexual behavior. If you feel that telling the child about sexual behaviors will increase the probability of his performing those behaviors, then you will probably embellish your discussion with many cautions and threats about the bad and nasty things that can happen. If you are going to say such things, then it might be better that the child be ignorant rather than informed and frightened or miserable.

Ignorance about sex is not a natural state and the choice of whether your child gets a sex education or not is really not a choice you have to make. TV, magazines, friends, and school all contribute to his information. The choice you have concerns whether or not your child will also have the benefit of his parents' information on the subject.

What kind of a balancing effect the parents' teachings will have on present and future sexual behavior depends upon the kind of rules implied by the parents. If these rules threaten punishments that could be used only if the parents found out about the behaviors, then the children will learn to keep secrets. If these rules threaten punishments for talking about sex at home, then the children will also learn to keep quiet.

It is impossible to administer consequences if you do not see the behaviors. Therefore, the best you can do as a parent is to encourage your child to tell you what's going on so that you can point out what the consequences might be.

## OBJECTIVES *chapter nine*

1.  What is the double benefit from a child's learning to do chores and develop everyday living habits?

2.  Describe how a check list can help in getting a child to keep his or her room clean.

3.  What is the disadvantage of using bedtime as a punishment for incorrect behavior?

4.  List three reasons why a child may refuse to go to sleep.

5.  What are two advantages of a graduated allowance?

6.  What are two reasons for procrastination?

7.  Give two reasons that public behavior exhibited by a child is sometimes different from his or her behavior at home.

# 10 / Teen-agers and Independence

**M**ost of the problems for the teen-ager exist because his parents have not yet adjusted to the fact that he is no longer a child. This lack of understanding is reflected primarily in the limited responsibilities and opportunities to perform as an adult that are given to him in the day-to-day activities of the family. A teen-ager's complaint that he has nothing to do should not be interpreted as a complaint about a lack of amusements but rather as a complaint about the lack of opportunity to perform tasks that are genuinely rewarded by the adult world and that he is prepared to do. Probably the quickest way to alienate him is to not take seriously his potential to contribute to what needs to be done in the family.

One of the reasons girls seem to survive adolescence with less turmoil than boys is probably that a girl's contributions to the family, particularly in terms of domestic chores, are taken advantage of at a much earlier age. The girl is a victim of discrimination, but it is the boy who suffers the most because of it in this growing-up period. Deprived of useful and contributing activities to perform, the boys contribute more than their share of school problems, automobile accidents, mental patients, and criminals.

The boy's masculinity in the American home somehow protects him from being useful. The lack of activity for a teen-ager may be as much a reason for teen-age depression as it is a result of depression. People who have nothing to do tend to complain most; they also tend to be the most troublesome.

Therefore, you must make plans, creative plans, for your child's adolescence. These plans should center around new responsibilities and activities that he is going to be allowed to do in and out of the home. The time has come to take off some of the protective wrapping and the restraining leashes.

### Waning Parental Influence

A great proportion of the parents' worries about their teen-ager is over his relationship with friends. Although teen-age crime is on the upswing, the teen-ager rarely commits a crime alone. Although rebellion is characteristic of his age, the teen-ager hardly ever rebels alone. And although adventure, change, and novelty are his watchwords, the teen-ager rarely seeks any of these by himself. The teen-ager is most at ease with his friends and enjoys their company in part because they reward a wide range of his behaviors and seldom reprimand, correct, or punish—which, by definition, means that they like him. When he is with them, he is free of parental pressure. There is little threat of reprimand or correction for breaking social rules, because now breaking social rules is seen as part of the adventure.

There are certainly taboos among teen-agers, and a strong social culture exists indicating what to wear and when to wear it and what to say and how to say it. Any parent of a teen-ager has seen the great concern that his son or daughter has when it seems that he is about to break one of these precious rules. But the rules are simple and few in number. And if the teen-ager must obey the rules, he can also enforce them among his peers. Because he is an enforcer of rules as well as a student of them, he finds the situation easy to bear—and seldom aversive. When he is with his peers, he enjoys many rewards provided by rules that he has come to agree with. He has also found a great deal of acceptance and little threat, little nagging, and very little punishment. So parents are no longer the only powerful influence in the lives of their teen-agers, and the parents are running out of time in which to exert their influence. If the teen-ager is to gain any more practice under the supervision of his parents, plans will have to be made quickly.

Parents have many reactions to finding out that they are no longer the only powerful influence in the life of their teen-ager, but a common complaint is that the teen-ager spends so much time with friends. The parents sometimes think he should be "doing something more worthwhile," which usually means "something that would be rewarded by me." But has such an activity actually been designated? And has there been a powerful reward planned or does the designation of an activity merely mean that the parents have decided to nag about something new?

Nagging about something new usually ends in failure to produce any change and also fills up the time so that there is no opportunity for good, rewarded behaviors. At this point the parents become fatalistic. Instead of using strategy sessions for planning, they develop habits that interfere with the opportunities for practice. These habits are described in this chapter.

The I'm-too-tired-to-do-any-more habit is sometimes characterized as parental depression. It usually comes from having no plan of consequences and practice, or it comes from attending so many behaviors that none of the plans is carried out. There seems to be so much the teen-ager hasn't learned yet, and there are so few years left. Often the parental reaction is to try to fix everything, comment on all errors, and provide few rewards ("he gets too much anyway")—and, after failing, the parent gets very "tired." The only energy he has left is for nagging.

To break this habit parents must focus on fewer of the teen-ager's behaviors and provide a great deal of social reward in place of the nagging. Some family policies can help this situation, and they are described here and in Chapter 11. But parents must guard against trying to do too much at first.

Sometimes the response of the parents to a growing teen-ager is to continue to provide practice and reward for childish behav-

## EXPERIMENT 29

### Help From Some Friends

Tom[40] was in a foster home for pre-delinquent boys who were getting into trouble too often. After several arrests, but before commitment to a reform school, many boys were assigned to this family-style program where teacher-parents, trained in behavioral approaches to problems, care for the 11- to 15-year-old boys.

A token economy allowed Tom and the other boys to earn points for their social, self-care and academic behaviors. The points could be turned in for the privilege of snacks, bike rides, shopping trips, or TV time.

At 13, Tom still had many speech problems that interfered with his academic and social activities. He had worked with a speech therapist but "just wouldn't try". So four other boys became the speech modifiers.

Each day the boys went over 70 cards with Tom. Each card had a word or picture that indicated a certain word, printed on it. The words represented four sounds Tom had trouble with: "ting" (he said "kuin" for "cutting"); "th" ("fum" for "thumb"); "r" ("fatho" for "father");

and "l" ("four" for "flower"). The boys worked on one problem at a time, using only half of the words in the cards which had to do with the problem.

The boys started with the "l". With eight one-problem words written down in front of them they watched for errors on those words as Tom went through all 70 cards. The first of the four boys to point out an error received 20 points in the token economy. Tom lost ten points of the 100 that were paid for attending the session. After the error had been pointed out the boy who had caught it would correct Tom until he had it right, then Tom would continue.

After six sessions with the "l" problem, the boys went on to the "r". After the 21st session they started working on pronouncing the "th", but with only one "therapist" present at a session. For the final problem, "ting", the boys received points when Tom was right rather than when they judged him wrong.

The graph in Figure 23 shows Tom's improvement. Even when the boys checked up on him 30 and 60 days after the treatment Tom's improvement had maintained.

ior. For example, they may still encourage him to dress on time and even disallow practice by selecting his clothes and watching the clock for him. They may continue to parcel out his allowance for his spending money but still decide on and buy everything

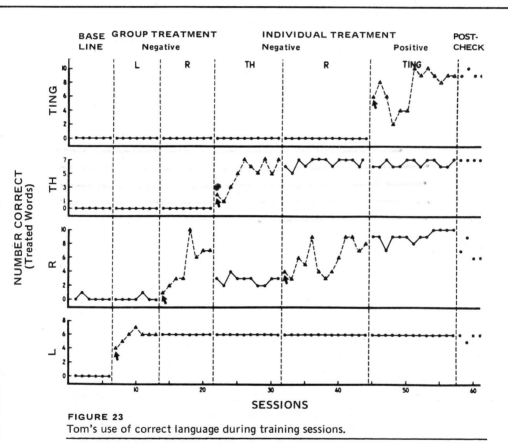

**FIGURE 23**
Tom's use of correct language during training sessions.

(Reprinted with permission of the **Journal of Applied Behavior Analysis.** Bailey, J.S., Timbers, G.D., Phillips, E.L., and Wolf, M.M. "Modification of articulation errors of pre-delinquents by their peers." **Journal of Applied Behavior Analysis.** 1971, 4, 269. Copyright 1971 by the Society for the Experimental Analysis of Behavior, Inc.)

that is meaningful (clothes, meals, school supplies, items for his room, and so on). Their excuse for this habit is usually that he has not yet learned the more adult behaviors perfectly, and, therefore, he cannot be allowed more responsibility.

The hesitation of the parents to demand new independence and responsibility may come from many sources. For example, it may be that new strategies are no longer being planned or that the risk in allowing the teen-ager to do "real and important" things may be too frightening to the parents. Or the parents may see the end of their responsibility for their children after the teens and therefore be reluctant to take this last step and then have nothing to do afterward.

To make things better for the teen-ager, parents sometimes continue rewards with no behavioral requests. Such activities reflect the "sacrificing parent habit," and they provide an unrealistic and cruelly misleading situation that does not prepare the teen-ager for the adult world. This habit is directly opposed to bringing that world into the life of the teen-ager. Thus, in dealing with the problems of teen-agers, emphasis must be placed upon realistic requests with realistic consequences—both positive and negative.

### Actions Speak Louder

One of the common errors in dealing with the teen-ager is to attend and react to his verbal descriptions of his behaviors and intentions rather than to plan your reactions and concern yourself with his performance. Such an error in strategy sometimes leads to a situation in which the teen-ager finds it easy to get through to you by making a remark about some absurd behavior that he has no intention of performing. At best, this strategy will be successful in rewarding good verbal behavior in the home but still have little effect on performance in the outside world. At worst, it will give selective attention to bad verbal behavior in the home while having no effect on behavior outside the home.

To get a teen-ager to "talk right" it is common for parents to sit down and talk to him when it seems that things have gone wrong. Such "little talks" teach him that if his parents want to talk to him, it is probably because he has somehow gotten into trouble. Announced little talks, then, are likely to be aversive situations. Moreover, a second disadvantage of the little talk is that it is meant to be a consequence. Threats are made, voices are raised, and generally the teen-ager gets a good talking-to. The good talking-to does not function well as a punishment because it is too far removed from the behavior and because it occurs so infrequently.

It is not surprising, therefore, that the talks have little effect on the behavior being discussed and that the teen-agers would rather avoid such talks. The parents' orientation is to keep the teen-ager out of trouble and see that nothing goes wrong rather than to allow him to grow up and to provide him with an incentive for things to go right.

Thus, if you can't seem to keep the teen-ager out of trouble, it may be best to avoid little talks. Instead develop a strategy that does not attempt to suppress the troublesome behavior but rather tends to reward good behaviors that might replace it. Begin to think of the things that the teen-ager *could do* to be good rather than the things he should *not do* to be good.

The fact that a teen-ager is good and quiet and that he is out of the way should not necessarily be interpreted as acceptable, for it may indicate that he is getting very little experience and practice at doing anything. A schoolteacher, for example, once said, "Oh, he is the best boy in the class. You hardly know he is there." It was the boy's lack of behavior that had impressed the teacher. Somewhere along the way the idea of teaching him new behaviors had been partly eroded by encouraging him to do nothing at all.

## Intentions as Actions

During the little talks and during strategy sessions it is tempting to state great intentions without specifying precisely what rules you will enforce. Such intentions, even when they concern a rule, usually concern a rule about verbal behavior only. For example, if one of your children curses, you may state that you are going to "swat him" if he ever says anything like that again. Of course, such an intention is impossible to fulfill; you will not always be present when he curses and the possibility of reprimanding him verbally rather than "swatting" him is very high. To state such an intention rewards the parents for having had a strategy session about the cursing yet allows them to do nothing specific in the future to reduce cursing. Thus, an intention is a statement set down in such general and sometimes emotional terms that it will never be carried out, whereas a rule is carefully thought out, written down, and adhered to at specified times.

## The Unembarrassed Parent

A parent is most vulnerable to being controlled by the bad behavior of his teen-ager in public. The teen-ager quickly learns that the parent is more easily embarrassed by his bad behavior than he is himself. This information can provide great leverage in day-to-day family activities.

It is because the parents influence their children so strongly by example that the consequences received by the child are effective on the parent. The more traditional way of expressing the situation would be to say that the parent "identifies" with the child—that is, the social consequences that the child receives may also have effects on the parent. The father, for example, knows that he is partially responsible for shaping the behavior of his children, and because he is painfully aware that a great deal of this behavior was determined by his example, he may be *personally* influenced by his son's success in sports. Here the child's behavior is obviously in control of the parent's reaction. The success or failure of the child is the primary influence in the parent's emotional reaction, whether or not he has the capacity to manipulate it.

In such a situation the child may become cynical when he realizes that his parent's special concern for him is really personal concern for a confirmation of success in raising him.

## Rewards for Teen-agers

RESPONSIBILITY AS REWARD AND PRACTICE / Now that your child has grown up to this age, what can be done with him? Here is a person who is probably better educated for his age than you were; and his situation—being all dressed up with nowhere to go—can be a source of frustration to him. Many demands have been made for him to educate himself, to learn new behaviors, and to learn about the-important activities that are going on in the adult world. Now that he is about to complete his education, what will he do with it? The general answer to that question should be that he will start practicing some of the tasks now. Could he be allowed to handle the family checking account? Could he be allowed to do the weekly shopping? Could a certain amount of money be allotted to him to take care of the yard? Could he be responsible for planning the family food budget? Could he be responsible for planning the budget for the maintenance and use of the car?

All these responsibilities are to some extent rewards as well as examples of good practice. But again it should be emphasized that the consequences, the rewards for the performance of these behaviors, must still be added.

PARENTAL ATTENTION AS A REWARD / Now that a large range of easily attainable social rewards is available outside the family, the parents' social rewards are not in great demand. The use of selective parental attention as a consequence will not be as effective as it was in earlier years. Parents now have competition, and strong competition it is. Furthermore, parents cannot be very efficient about giving attention, because they love their teen-ager and cannot totally ignore and reject him for his bad behavior. In the long run, they will probably forgive any infringement upon the rules. Peers, on the other hand, in spite of all their clubs and their promises will never be that loyal. The experience of being deserted by friends has repeatedly proved that point to the teen-

---

## EXPERIMENT 30

### Group Contingencies

**Music.** Two seventh- and two eighth-grade home economics classes[41] presented very noisy situations. With sewing machines on one side of the classroom, materials on another, and tables in between, the girls carried on a very high level of clatter and chatter.

The experimenter installed a microphone along with other equipment which measured the noise level in the room. If the amount of noise dropped to a reasonable level, a radio tuned to a favorite station came on and played softly. When the noise level went up the radio went off.

The girls quieted down. The noise level which turned off the radio was exceeded 40% of the time during baseline but less than 10% of the time when the radio was contingent on quiet.

**Free Time.** The new teacher, Mr. M[42], was having trouble managing the seventh-grade math and geography classes. As one remedy for the problem, he used a rotary-type file of 18 cards. He announced, "By obeying the class rules, you can earn [up to] 18 minutes of free time at the end of class. Each time any student violates a rule, I will flip one of these cards and the entire class will have one less minute of free time." Observations of the eight most disruptive students showed good behavior jumped from 30% to 80%. While the group contingency still provided the best results, good behavior occurred 70% of the time even when Mr. M made each student earn his own points for free time.

**"Deals".** Six ninth graders[43] were poor students, and with good cause: they attended school only about 30% of the time! A counselor tried to arrange for good reasons for attendance at school by the students by contacting people who controlled rewards for those six. He arranged some contingencies which the students called "deals". Deals made attendance necessary for: access to a pool hall, use of fancy clothes, money, weekend privileges, and time with a girl friend. Deals were in effect for seven weeks and attendance averaged over 80%, dropping back to 55% when the counselor was called away for two weeks! Good reasons can get good behavior.

ager. Therefore, after weighing the risks of doing what his peers want him to do versus what his parents want him to do, the teen-ager will often favor his peers. He knows that his parents will still be there and will eventually forgive him; he also knows that his peers may not be there or may not forgive him easily.

So the parents' position has changed, and their function as social rewarders is becoming weaker. But a new role is appearing —the role of the bystander. The bystander points out how the consequences and the behaviors of the teen-ager are related, how the rebuffs of his friends and acquaintances are related to his behaviors, and why certain behaviors resulted in certain experiences. The parents no longer provide all consequences, but they can now interpret consequences while the teen-ager remains at home those last few years, benefiting from his own practice and experience.

THE FAT CATS / Don't be too discouraged by the loss of your social attention as a strong reward. Your teen-ager is still dependent upon you for many concrete things. As a case in point, consider the rebellious teen-ager who acts on the false premise that he is perfectly capable of making it on his own. Usually his parents have misled him into believing that this is the case by providing most of the essentials of life absolutely free. You too could make it on your own if you earned $25 a week from a part-time job and still had parents to provide the other $50 or $60 a week that it would take for room, board, clothing, books, tuition, and so on.

So the false notion of easy rebellion comes to some extent from being a "fat cat." This label refers to a person who does not have a great income but who is not required to spend even a part of his small income on any of the essentials of life and therefore ends up with a great deal of money in his pocket because he is being carried along. The situation can develop if parents fail to make realistic demands on the teen-ager's pocketbook. Perhaps he has not been allowed to contribute to the family either financially or otherwise in return for the conveniences and advantages he continues to enjoy at home. It is unrealistic and cruel training to allow a teen-ager to come and go in the family household reaping all the benefits while paying nothing in return.

MATCHING FUNDS AND GRADUATED ALLOWANCES / If more financial demands are to be made on the teen-ager, then a better means of making and using money will have to be provided. Allowances tend to be the major source of income for children and teen-agers. Part-time jobs are available to them, but ordinarily even if they hold such jobs they still receive a great deal of money from their parents.

A graduated allowance pays off a variable amount of money depending upon the behavior of the teen-ager. It uses the traditional allowance, which was guaranteed and usually unrelated to performance, as a new means of applying reasonable and effective consequences. Certain responsibilities that have specific behavioral definitions are assigned to each teen-ager (or child) and listed on a chart. Each time the teen-ager fulfills one of his responsibilities a mark is made to indicate the event. Each mark is deemed worth a certain amount of money, and at the end of the week the marks are counted and the total is paid to the teen-ager. You might set a minimum amount of allowance so that you never completely deprive the teen-ager and a maximum so that a burst of good performance does not break your own pocketbook. Keep in mind, however, that to some extent such minimums and maximums erode the effectiveness of the rule.

Try to set the value of the points high enough to provide some substantially higher amount of money to the teen-ager each week than has ordinarily been the case in the past. This increase is an extra motivation, and, as you will see, it does not have to be more expensive for you.

As the money comes rolling in for your teen-ager under the

new system, begin to provide new ways for him to spend it besides for his own amusement and stomach. For example, you might consider a matching-funds program for buying his own clothes, which will give him a sense of responsibility in selecting clothes and a greater appreciation of their cost and possibly their care. Expenses for birthday gifts, the family car, and entertainment would, of course, come from this new large graduated allowance. So as you enter this new system be sure that the teen-ager is required to bear the expense of necessities as well as luxuries. For example, if he is given a matching fund for clothes, be sure that he puts up half the money for underpants and socks as well as for fancy new shirts.

## The Family Car

As a person gets into his middle and late teens there is usually a great family eruption over his use (or misuse) of the family car. This problem usually begins with an argument over whether he is old enough to learn to drive and continues about the lessons themselves.

TEACHING DRIVING / Teaching your teen-ager to drive can be done safely and well, but it will require a shaping and fading process. Thus, there is no reason even to start the engine of a car during the first training sessions. It would be better to sit next to your son or daughter and pretend that corners were coming up, stoplights were changing, gears needed to be shifted, and so on. Two hours of familiarizing the student with where the various important instruments are would not be excessive.

When you and your student feel that he is responding confidently in the pretended situations, you might plan his first real lesson. Many of the accidents that the novice experiences occur because the teacher has confused him about where he is to go, turn, or stop. For the first lesson, plan with your student before you start exactly where the car is to be driven, what turns are to be made, and how you will return. This briefing will avoid hectic and confusing moments when neither you nor your student knows what is about to happen.

Begin with a simple plan such as driving around the block and repeat it several times before adding another driving course. Also repeat this plan at the beginning of every lesson. Gradually expand the plan of where you are going to go *before* each lesson. Do not jump from driving around the block to driving down Main Street. Possibly a second step would be driving around the block so that left turns rather than right ones have to be made.

If you begin teaching the elements of driving in this gradual manner, you may find that your son's or daughter's learning to drive will not be such a traumatic experience for either of you.

Now is the time to dispel the idea that driving a car is nothing but fun and games. Set up a matching-funds program for gasoline and service of the car. Also set up a matching-funds program for the insurance and driver's license expenses. As soon as he gets his license, reward him with a responsibility that he can perform with the car—for example, driving the smaller children to music lessons or to school.

USE OF THE CAR AS A CONSEQUENCE / Usually the use of the family car can be an effective consequence in shaping other behaviors. The difficulty is that the teen-ager's need for the car varies from time to time. Thus, the effectiveness of car use as a consequence has some of the same difficulties as the use of TV time. You never know when he is really going to want it. It may be necessary, therefore, to set up a chart that keeps a running total of the amount of time that your teen-ager may use the car. This chart may state specifically that certain times of the week are excluded and that he can only make use of his earned time during other periods of the week. For example, you may know in advance that you need the car every Thursday, Friday, and Sunday night and that there is no chance of his cashing in any of his earned time on those evenings. This condition should be stated on the chart.

To withhold the use of the car as a punishment has the same disadvantage as allowing its use as a reward. You never know how effective this deprivation will be on a particular day. So if the negative side of the coin is to be used, it should be used in conjunction with the chart just described. Note, however, that this punitive arrangement will at times be tied up with the teen-ager's availability to friends. You are stepping on fairly sacred soil and should work out a rule that everyone understands.

POOR DRIVING HABITS / A review of the consequences for driving habits sometimes explains a great deal about that behavior. Who pays for poor driving habits? Who benefits from them? The answer to the first question should be that the driver pays for replacing balding tires, insurance, and maintenance through his graduated allowance or whatever. Bad driving has the same benefits as any other attention-getting behavior. If bad driving is not being used to get through to the parents, then most of the attention is coming from people beyond the parents' control. At this point the only consequences left to the parents are negative ones. The consequences can be effective, but they are difficult to apply. A specific definition of bad behavior with the car will have to be used and a somewhat drastic measure will have to be used as a negative consequence.

Removing the driving privilege is usually the first negative consequence that comes to mind. The exact length of time the privilege should be withheld and whether or not chores done with the car should be dispensed with are things that must be spelled out to avoid arguments.

Certain physical controls are possible, of course, and if the parents want to take the trouble, the controls can be very effective. A speed governor is available from any auto supply store. A better solution might be to place more logical restrictions on the

time the teen-ager is allowed to have the car and on the distances
he can go. Of course, consequences would have to be stated in
these rules. Still, the most reasonable rules, which will in the long
run control bad driving behavior, are those that give the expense
of car operation to the teen-ager.

## Work

GUFF / It may seem strange to parents of teen-agers that the
common complaint of disrespect has not yet been discussed in this
chapter. Many parents complain of such behavior and even complain that their teen-ager is trying to punish them. In many cases
disrespect *is* a punishment—that is, it is meant to suppress the
behavior of the person to whom it is directed. Usually the behavior it is designed to suppress is some request of the parent, and
therefore a more accurate label than "disrespect" is "guff"—an
effort to put off work.

The fact that a teen-ager might consider getting out of work
as a reward usually indicates that he pays no particular price for
not performing as was requested. That is, guff is a sign that the
parents do not require the teen-ager to do his own work. They
do not require that he take logical consequences for his lack of
performance. For example, if he manages to give enough guff that
his parents will stop requesting that he make his bed, then the
logical consequence of having an unmade bed might reduce the
frequency of that particular kind of guff. A teen-ager who can
look forward to having his mother make his bed—if he can just
get out of doing the chore for the time being—is likely to use
guff. So it is not the guff that should be dealt with. It is the
consequences given for failing to fulfill requests and the consequences given *for* fulfilling parental requests. Usually the teen-
ager is giving "all that guff" for two reasons. He receives no
particular reward for respecting the requests of his parents and no
particular discomfort for failing to respect their requests.

ASSIGNMENTS AT HOME / Much teen-age grouchiness and depression is described, even by the teen-ager, as caused by the lack of something to do. This complaint and the resulting grouchiness can be taken care of temporarily by amusement, but amusements usually don't last long.

You are at an advantage if you think about work assignments at home before your child becomes a teen-ager, because it is more difficult to assign duties and responsibilities to him if he has never had many to do before. Even, however, if the duties have never been his before, you should start.

The system you are most likely to use is one of graduated allowances and duties (assigned individual jobs) checked off on a chart. The plan should include a liberal amount of responsibility concerning when the work is to be done, how money for the expenses of the job is to be spent, and so on. Remember that if the teen-ager is to become interested, he will have to be assigned the interesting parts of the job as well as the tedious ones. Also consider the rewarding and productive combination of paying off a lot of money while giving him more responsibility for his own expenses.

THE OUTSIDE JOB / The older teen-ager can almost always find an outside job that will provide good experience and serve as another step in growing up. Such a job provides excellent therapy for the teen-ager who seems to have time on his hands and uses this time as an opportunity for bad behavior; it is also effective for the teen-ager who is depressed and feels that he is not doing anything worthwhile.

An outside job has the advantage of making less work for the parent concerning strategies, charts, and payoffs. It has the disadvantage of leaving the home chores without a potential reward (the teen-ager gets his money elsewhere now), and this independence may become evident in his unwillingness to perform responsibilities at home.

Some of the problems of independence can be solved by giving him more responsibility for his own expenses. This would be done if he were expanding his allowance by doing chores at home. But remember that if he is to pay his own way just like an adult, then he will ask to be allowed to go his own way just like an adult. It would be unfair to ask him to buy his own clothes and then insist on going with him to make sure he gets the right thing. He will have to learn for himself what the right thing is.

More of the limits of this independence will have to be spelled out at the crucial time when the teen-ager starts his first outside job. He is bound to feel more independence and deserves more—but how much more? Arguments about his independence

---

## EXPERIMENT 31

### Rewarding Employment

"$100 job locater fee will be paid to any person who provides information about a job opening which results in the employment of one of our job applicants . . ."[44]

The ad capitalized on the use of rewards in job finding. It was prompted by a survey that revealed that 71% of those questioned got their job leads from friends or relatives who had themselves been hired by the firm. Sixty-three percent of these people knew of a specific opening and passed it along. If that was the job source then it seemed reasonable to encourage the source.

The ad produced ten times as many job placements when compared with an ad that read:

"We currently have applicants seeking employment in . . . If you know of a position . . . please call."

Attendance at self-help groups for welfare recipients[45] averaged three persons until items donated from the community were used as rewards for attendance. Toys to be taken home to the children, furniture, appliances, rugs, and kitchen utensils were available. The person attending was allowed to select one item at each meeting. Average attendance increased to 15 persons and relevant problems concerning jobs, health care and welfare services were able to be discussed **and followed up** from meeting to meeting because attendance was reliable.

usually boil down to a disagreement about his hours. As with most arguments with teen-agers, it would be better if there were an unhurried, private discussion between the parents before the running battles continue. These strategy sessions should also determine what chores and duties are still to be assigned to the working teen-ager. An agreement will have to be reached about a special effort to encourage and reward (socially) these chores. The agreement can be complicated if you are planning to ask for both "rent" and performance of chores. Is your particular combination of chores and rent fair?

### Eating and Dressing Habits

Many parents complain of a deterioration in the eating and dressing habits of their teen-agers. Such changes are somewhat surprising in the sense that the behavior in most cases was better at an earlier age than it is now. The deterioration in habits may occur because the good behaviors are not rewarded; the "errors" may have crept in because they tend to draw a lot of attention.

Bad eating and dressing habits are usually attention-getting behaviors, but they also signal a possible lack of positive reward for good behaviors that happen. After you have planned for the influence of attention (for good behavior) and the lack of it (for bad behavior), you might consider the matching-funds program described above to develop more interest in dress.

If eating habits are a problem, then possibly it is time to have teen-age peers over more often to bring their pressure to bear. One mother, for example, complained about her daughter's eating habits and language at dinnertime. Between the poor eating habits and bad language, the family found mealtimes rather unappetizing. After seriously considering the consequences and reasons for the behavior, the mother herself conceived a plan using peers, and she carried it out very successfully. The next time one of her daughter's friends came for dinner, the mother began to act in a peculiar way. She suddenly developed many of the eating habits her daughter had when they ate without company. Her language was also atrocious. The friend was surprised and the daughter stunned. But, she received a new insight and an education when she said, "Oh mother, you can't imagine how terrible I felt when you said, 'pass the _____ _____ potatoes'." "Yes I can," her mother said, "it's the same feeling I had every other night this week. And I guess you know that feeling too, now."

Another factor in poor eating and dressing habits may be that the teen-ager has not been allowed to share in some of the more crucial aspects of the activity concerned. For example, it is difficult to see why a teen-ager should be interested in how he is dressed if his parents insist on selecting all the clothes that he buys and wears. If this is the case, the parents are seriously misusing their parental control. They are preventing the teen-ager from practicing an adult behavior that he must learn fairly well in the very immediate future if he is to be a successful adult. Eating and dressing habits are probably the first crucial areas in which the parents must learn to give their children complete responsibility for some decisions. If they wish to keep the behavior within some range of reasonableness, possibly a matching-funds program of the kind described in this chapter would be helpful.

## Rebellion

When a teen-ager refuses to go along with the rules his parents have set up and gets angry and aggressive when repeatedly asked to obey these rules, then the situation is usually described as rebellion. There's a song in the play, *The Fantastics*, which says of the children, "They did it because we said, 'No'." The challenge of being told "no" fits in all too nicely with the boredom that may be produced by being treated like a child. Bored with old and childish rules, the teen finds an adventure in a fight with the parents over a "no". This situation may indicate that the rules evidently do not provide enough incentive for good behaviors and, as is often the case, the rules may not provide opportunities for the teen-ager to show what he can do. The teen-ager often expresses his feeling about this condition by saying that everything is "boring", and challenging the "no's" relieves the boredom.

It is not necessary to add rewards to relieve boredom and restriction. As a matter of fact, part of the problem may be that the rewards are coming in for no particular effort, which, in itself, is boring. A king may not be restricted, but he may be bored for reasons similar to the teen-ager's reasons—too much has been given without any request or price.

It may be difficult to backtrack now and ask that a teen-ager work for things that were freely given to him before, but perhaps the only way a king can be happy is to make him work like everyone else. If this change is made, however, isn't it adding even more restrictions to the teen-ager? The answer to this question depends on the rules and work you set up for him. If you are willing to assign only drudgery, which no one wants to do, then in a way there are more restrictions. If, on the other hand, you can add more important responsibilities, then you might expand and enrich the teen-ager's opportunities. His job should be not just washing the car, but taking it to the garage for maintenance—and having the money to do it with. Not just cleaning up his room and hanging up clothes, but a matching fund for clothes and room accessories of his choice. Not just mowing the lawn, but a budget for care of the yard.

Will he make mistakes, waste a little money, buy different clothes than you would, do strange things to the lawn? You bet he will! But he will learn. And everyone who is capable will be a participant in the family operation.

Untapped capability is usually at the core of boredom (on the teen-ager's side) and restriction (as laid down by the parent). Boredom cannot be done away with overnight, but a new rule that shows respect for the fact that a teen-ager is not ten years old can help.

## Dating

If both the teen-ager and his parents are honest about dating, the parents can provide him with a great deal of helpful information. Unfortunately, the most common circumstance is one in which the teen-ager is playing "Better safe (and silent) than sorry" and his parents are playing "Let's keep him out of trouble." So again the emphasis is on warnings and advice about bad behavior with verbal reprimands as the consequence for reporting any behavior. This situation is not disastrous; it is normal, and we have all survived it.

But if parents would like to be of real help, they might teach what they know about successful dating behaviors—not just manners and things that will lead to their idea of a successful evening but also things that will lead to the teen-ager's idea of a successful evening.

For example, usually the biggest worry a person has on a date or out with friends is whether or not he or she is going to be liked. If that's true of your teen then it must be true of his friends as well. Therefore, the best way he or she can reward others on a date is to let them know that he likes them. Often we are so worried about acting "right" so that they will like us that we forget that they have the same motivations. Part of acting "right" is to let other people know you like them with praise, attention, and encouragement.

Also, you could point out to your daughter that girls really dress for the approval of other girls and that sincere compliments to other girls will always be appreciated. This advice might even help her in selecting her own clothes. You could also point out to your son that boys are expected to plan the evening. Your son could be helped to have a better evening if this were discussed along with all the talk about driving the car. Also point out that attention, as a reward, is just as important between friends as it used to be between you and your teen-ager. He must learn to use plenty of this with his date. When the date has a miserable evening, it is usually because his planning was poor or he failed to pay attention to her.

## The Rude Awakening

Between parent and teen-ager the rules and consequences of give and take are sometimes not in effect, but in the rest of the real world they are. Usually the teen-ager is faced with an eventual rude awakening that the world will not pay off as easily as loving parents do. Somewhere along the way the teen-ager will also have to become a believer in the reward and consequence system. He must believe not only in the rules that affect him but also in using such rules when he makes a serious attempt to influence someone else. It is time he learned to dispense social rewards as well as to accept them. And he must also learn to dispense social rewards purposefully at times.

The advice that parents give the teen-ager should concern not only how his behavior is related to the consequences *he* receives but how his behavior works as a consequence for *others*.

Among the rewards the teen-ager uses to encourage others is his own social availability. Friends are the most important aspect of his life, and the measure of a friend, at this age, is the amount of time he can be counted on to be available. A teen-ager's moodiness about "being with" so-and-so is, therefore, a dangerous part of the adolescent disposition. As the teen-ager's parents often know, his friends are more fickle than he believes. When the social rewards stop coming, when your child is not so available, when his attention turns away momentarily to someone else, his friends are likely to turn their attention away quickly too. It's not too early to begin to teach your child the rules of human behavior that you are using. This is an important message for the parents to convey in conversations about consequences.

## OBJECTIVES   *chapter ten*

1.  Why are teenagers generally more
    at ease with their friends than with
    their parents?

2.  What is a common parental reaction
    to discovering that they are no
    longer the only powerful influence
    on their teenager's life?

3.  What is a cause of parental depression?

4.  What is the sacrificing parent habit?

5.  What are two disadvantages of hold-
    ing "little talks" when things go
    wrong?

6.  What is the difference between an
    intention and a rule?

7.  What is a "fat cat"?

8.  What are two common reasons for
    teenagers giving "guff"?

9.  What is meant by the "rude awaken-
    ing"?

# 11 / The Successful Family

To make the design of consequences run smoothly in the family some general arrangements of rules may be necessary. A system for ensuring the use of concrete rewards may be needed, and some specific arrangements about family cooperation with social rewards may be helpful. Such arrangements for improving the success of behavioral strategies may be as specific as a token economy or as general as parent-child friendships.

## The Token Economy

Often it is impossible to have an effective reward at hand for maintaining day-to-day activities. Sometimes the social rewards that we ordinarily use are not given because we are just not in the mood or because the social reward is really not appropriate as a consequence for the activity.

Most of these activities are chores or other work details that all of us must learn to do with some consistency. They also happen to be behaviors that are, in the real world, paid off in a rather concrete manner and are not supported entirely by social reward. For most adults, concrete rewards for work, personal appearance, and the appearance of the home come at long intervals. We have learned that we can expect the rewards sometime in the future.

But for children who have not yet learned that they must take care of their room or that they have responsibilities in the family for washing dishes, preparing meals, taking care of clothes, and so on, these concrete rewards must come more frequently and come right after the behaviors themselves.

A system can be constructed that will allow payoffs for individual behaviors of the children. This system should not be used to bribe children for getting the work done but rather to compensate them for contributing to the work and the domestic necessities of the family. Thus, they must learn, as they will have to learn later, that in order for family life to run smoothly they must put in an effort and for this effort they will be given their proper share of the family income. In this sense, family life is an economy in which there is an exchange of activities on the part of the members and a compensation for those activities.

Psychologists have come to call the system described above a token economy because in much of the early research done on this concept tokens were used to represent the payoff. The traditional American idea of an allowance is a kind of token-economy system, but usually it does not employ a strict behavioral rule stating that portions of the allowance will be given only if certain behaviors occur. The result of this lack of rules is that allowance is guaranteed or is given at the discretion of the parents. Consequently, the child's approach often is not to work but merely to time his request for his allowance according to the whims and moods of his parents.

The child may thus do his chores and other domestic activities only after nagging and coercion, and without much incentive from the allowance system. To a great extent, then, your first attempt at a token-economy system in your home might be merely to correct the way in which you dispense the allowance that you now give. You will probably end up giving a good deal more of an allowance than you expected, but you might not regret that too much if the child deserves it. As a first step, set up a chart on your kitchen bulletin board. List the behavior and domestic activities that you expect from each of the children in the left-hand column. See that these domestic chores are really a meaningful need of the family so that the children receive genuine responsibilities, not make-work duties.

When you first construct your chart, it would be best to use the child's suggestion as to which domestic responsibilities should be placed on it. In this way your estimate of his probabilities of performance will be low enough in order to ensure that some portion of his allowance will come through each week. Later in the progress of your token economy, you may wish to change some of the behavioral requirements represented on the chart. Let the other columns represent days of the week, and put the children on an honor system for placing a mark in the correct box if they have done the chore for that day. At a predetermined time each week, remove the chart, count the points, and pay the children their weekly allowance. Suppose you are paying a nickel for each mark on the chart. Lay the chart on the table so that the younger children can get a close look at the result of the week's work; for children under seven, have all the money in nickels and place each nickel on each mark on the chart so that the child understands why he receives just that many nickels. During the first week of this new allowance system you may have to pay off the allowance each day or every other day so that the children understand and begin to believe in the meaning of the marks on the chart.

As soon as the child has the nickels, you must provide an immediate opportunity for him to use them to buy something that he would like to have. You cannot assume that the nickels are any more meaningful to the child than any other kind of metal unless he has an opportunity to cash them in. The first danger point in using a token-economy system is that you are likely to attempt to coerce the child into saving up for a shopping trip rather than taking him out with his first few nickels and letting him buy the things *he* wants. In the early weeks it is important to convince the child that the "tokens" are really worth something. So make the shopping trip early. Later, the child will come up with the idea of saving.

As the child learns to save his nickels for shopping and as the

---

## EXPERIMENT 32

### A Token Economy

Mr. B[46] had to handle 25 kids in a combination fifth-and sixth-grade classroom. The children each liked different activities and it was difficult for Mr. B to remember how to reward each of his students. He started the year off in the usual manner but kept careful records of assignments completed. (These first six weeks served as a baseline to compare to later performance when he planned to use a token economy.) He began by listing point values to be paid by the students for the privileges usually available in a classroom: sharpening pencils (13 points for fifth graders, 20 for sixth), sports activities (40 points for fifth graders, 60 for sixth), listening to records (2 points for fifth graders, 5 for sixth), checking the grade book, special writing on the blackboard, etc.

The students **earned** points in several ways: correctly completing assigned classroom and homework papers (6 to 12 points); engaging in morning study behavior (5 points); bringing food for animals (1 to 10 points); being tidy (1 to 2 points); standing quietly in the lunch line

(2 points); and others. Students could also lose points for fighting, cheating, eating in class, etc.

Most of the points were earned in completing assignments. At the beginning of class students graded their papers, brought them to Mr. B for points, and recorded their points on individual record forms. He then recorded them in his grade book.

For 75 days, points were exchanged for privileges on Monday morning. There was a student banker for each privilege who then submitted the list to Mr. B. He found that students worked hardest for points when Monday was coming up, so he varied the day of exchange unpredictability during the rest of the year (called "Token II" in Figure 24).

At one stage, Mr. B told the class that points for assignments would no longer count. Points would have to be earned by the other behaviors and by being quiet. Assignment completion dropped to the level of the beginning baseline period (see "Quiet Behavior" in Figure 24). After that experience, Mr. B kept his Token II system going for the rest of the year.

weeks progress and the tallies on the week's chart become more numerous, it is tempting to fine the child for bad behavior and remove points or nickels. If you do, you take away some of the confidence the child has that he will be rewarded for the points that appear on the chart. Do not undermine his confidence in the

**FIGURE 24**
Percent of homework and classwork completed when Mr. B used token economies.

(Reprinted with permission of the **Journal of Applied Behavior Analysis.**
McLaughlin, T.F., and Malaby, J. "Intrinsic reinforcers in a classroom token economy." **Journal of Applied Behavior Analysis.** 1972, 5, 265. Copyright 1972 by the Society for the Experimental Analysis of Behavior, Inc.)

economy by establishing a policy that says the government can
make the money worthless any time it wishes. If you are still
convinced that some punishments are necessary, use something
irrelevant to the token-economy system.

Once the token economy is firmly established, other incentives can be added. The most important of these is probably the
contingent promotion. This procedure allows the duties on the
chart to be changed, improved, and modified as the child's performance improves. If he performs well on some of the more
simple and tedious chores, he might be promoted to a better set of
duties.

Contingent promotions are an important addition to the
token economy because they represent improvements in expectation and respect that the parent has with regard to the child's
capabilities. So if no promotions occur in the token economy,
then to some extent that system fails to do its job, because the
children are not growing up to new responsibilities. Such an
economy may maintain an improved level of performance of the
old chores, but this is not the only purpose the system can serve.

For example, a token-economy program was developed with
one mother that provided an incentive for her son's completion of
chores. After the system was applied for several weeks, the son
complained that some of the things he was required to do were
"kid's stuff." Putting waste baskets and garbage sacks outside the
house was particularly unpleasant to him. Because of his attitude,
a great deal of nagging, procrastination, and general unpleasantness took place concerning this task. So a contingent promotion
procedure was set up. The procedure provided that if the boy
successfully performed the task for fifteen straight days without
verbal coercion from his mother, he would be promoted to a new
task, washing the car. The chart would then be changed and the
job of removing waste baskets would be given to a younger
member of the family. The older son looked forward eagerly to
this possible change of events because he liked doing anything

with the car; the younger son welcomed an additional task because he had fewer opportunities than his brother did to perform duties to get tokens from the system.

The rule was set up so that if the boy completed only some portion of the fifteen days without failure, he would start counting from the beginning again until he got fifteen straight days of performance. Each day, of course, paid off with the usual tokens. Thus, performance always paid off, but particularly good performance paid a bonus in the form of a desirable change in the system.

## Family Strategy

Much of the time, a behavioral strategy about one child needs cooperation from the father, mother, and a sibling. Giving reward for such cooperation is difficult. What at one point seems to be a behavioral problem of a specific child may in reality be a problem of supporting the correct reactions of your spouse or of siblings. Here we find ourselves at another level of strategy; we must reward cooperation from other members of the family. This problem involves some of the same basic rules discussed before: a clear statement of the rules, an effective reward, and a simple, straightforward procedure for presenting the reward by those rules.

All members of the family involved have to be at the strategy session at which the rule is stated, for the rule not only specifies the behavior of the child that you are going to try to train but also specifies the behavior of those who are going to dispense the consequences. Again, a shaping procedure is involved and it may seem that you are a long way from solving the original problem. Remember that one of the benefits of this shaping procedure will be to make more effective (and more pleasant) human beings out of the other members of the family.

Fathers are usually the quickest to agree to the suggestion that a rule should involve a consequence. They usually think of themselves as practical people with a great spirit for practical rules but with a limited amount of time to spend enforcing those rules. Therefore, there will be differences between mothers and fathers even when they agree on the rule. The difference may be that the mother will be around to carry out the rule and the father will not. In constructing rules the parents will have to consider whether the father is likely to be present when the rule is needed. If it is likely that he will not be there, then he should be much more willing to compromise and cooperate with the mother's strategy.

This kind of arbitrary compromise is difficult for an American male and is a hard marital adjustment. Therefore, in early strategy sessions give priority to problems where both parents can get practice at using behavioral rules. Evening meals, homework, neatness, and sibling relationships are areas in which the father can take his full share of supporting the rules.

Normally the child's solution to the differences between his parents is to play one set of rules for his father against another set of rules for his mother. This divide-and-conquer approach can be extremely effective if there are no rules that both parents have agreed to enforce. The divide-and-conquer solution of the child is even more dangerous because it tends to magnify differences between the parents, so that when the child tries some rule testing he will always have one person on his side. Such alliances are difficult; they are never stable and always involve some unhappy conflict.

Many times the strategy session, rather than resolving conflicts, is subverted to discussing either marital problems or broad and poorly defined characteristics of the children. Be careful that your strategy session does not deteriorate into this kind of gripe session. Much of the difficulty arises from the fact that the strategy sessions have been used to agree on an attitude rather than on a simple, enforceable rule. Focus discussion on a particular behavior and its consequences rather than on speculation about how the behavior was shaped up by your spouse or how it is really a manifestation of some great general problem or attitude.

Problems can be further simplified if the father and mother give an honest report of the strategy session to the child when they state the rule. Do not tell a child that you and your spouse are in complete agreement if the truth is that you have reached a compromise. To tell a child that parents at times must compromise will not weaken the effectiveness of the rules, for rules remain effective as long as they are enforced by both parties. In other words, as long as a child understands that he cannot exploit this compromise by tempting one parent into waiving the rule, then the fact that the parents sometimes disagree is not difficult for the child to deal with and is not difficult for the parents to tolerate in raising the child.

FATHERS / In the role of family leader the father is most likely to be misused by being asked to serve as judge of the court of last resort. To say, "Wait till your father comes home and we'll see," or to agree to the request of a child "If Daddy says yes" is to allow opportunities for the child to play one parent against the other. The court of last resort should be the strategy session between father and mother—not a unilateral decision made by father, which may be perceived by the child as having veto power over the mother.

If some kind of "courtroom" behavior has begun, it may be necessary to use several strategy sessions to ask important questions about the differences between the consequences available from the father and the consequences available from the mother. "Are there differences in the probability of punishment?" "Why?" "For what behaviors?" "Are there differences between the parents as to the probability that they will give money?" "Why?" "For what behaviors?"

If these questions are raised in the strategy session, there may be an opportunity to bring about agreement and compromise. In most families, however, the mother provides most of the consequences all day and the father comes home to a worked-over situation. Not only is the situation well worked over, but the father may be rather worked over himself and feel that he has made his contribution for the day.

In the situation above, agreement and compromise may not have much meaning, because the father either is absent or feels that his responsibility is over for the day. Nevertheless, he *will* give out consequences. They may not be the obvious ones of disciplining the children, but, as was pointed out at the beginning of this book, consequences are inevitable.

The father's consequences may be obscure for several reasons. For example, his expectations may be higher—he may feel that the children can brush their own teeth without being told to do so or praised for having finished. It may look as if he just doesn't care, but in reality he has come to treat the children as if they were responsible for the activity. Possibly his lack of response is correct. At this point a strategy session could be helpful. Because the father tends to give fewer consequences as well as less direction, he becomes the parent of few words and therefore provides less warning of impending punishment. If this is the case, the children are likely to be more cautious with him. He seems to have better control over them. The better control may come partly from his habit of not giving much warning, but it also comes from the fact that he is not around as much and thus his presence is a novelty. Possibly there is something here for the mother to learn about nagging and warnings. Also, there may be something for the father to learn about cooperating with the mother's rules because she must deal with the children so much more.

RELATIVES / Relatives have a way of providing a set of rules and consequences all their own. In most cases there is no reason to correct these differences: they occur rather infrequently, and they are characteristic of life, for there will always be some individuals whose rules and consequences conflict with those of the parents.

There are long-term situations, however, in which relatives living with the family will have to be given at least an observer role in the strategy sessions, and this may create difficulties. Most parents feel that relatives should not take an active part in the first processes of a family session—that is, in the designation of what behaviors will be changed—but rather that they should cooperate in applying the strategies to be used on the behaviors that the parents designate important.

Concrete rewards and privileges can easily remain in the control of the parents. So when strategies are carried out using these consequences, the parents are in control. When the strategy involves attention-getting behavior, social rewards are crucial. In order to get an aunt in residence to refrain from giving attention to tantrums, she will have to be in on the strategy sessions in which the extinction procedure is worked out, and she will have to know about the good behaviors she is supposed to support. If she is aware of both sides of this strategy, she may be some help.

If you cannot get the aunt to cooperate and you do not want to throw her out, there's still hope. Don't give up the strategy. Children do learn to discriminate, as is evident when a child plays one parent against the other. It is harder on the child to have a stubborn aunt, but he can learn that tantrums don't work on his parents although they do on his aunt. The tantrums will be a bit hard on the old girl, but if she's going to insist on applying her own rules, then *she* gets the logical consequences: if she insists on supporting tantrums, then she gets tantrums. If you don't support tantrums but would rather support helpful and more pleasant talk by attending that, then, in the long run, you will have that. So even if you have a problem with relatives, keep your rule consistent and you will see some improvement.

SIBLINGS / In the United States there is a common assumption about the equality of siblings—parents seem to think it only fair that all the children be treated alike. In some respects this attitude is legitimate, but in many ways it ignores the real differences between children. Children are bound to have different friends, different physical limitations, and different interests and abilities. Children are well aware of them, and for the parents to tell children that they will be treated as if differences did not exist is to lay the groundwork for much misunderstanding. An honest and realistic strategy is always best. A younger child asks why he can't stay up as late as his older brother and asserts that the whole situation is unfair. Rather than making excuses continually in order to hide the fact, it would be better to tell him that his older brother may stay up later because he does not need as much sleep.

The same approach might be applied to situations in which one sibling demands that he constantly accompany another even when his age makes it inappropriate for him to do so. If a younger child never has to make friends because he can always depend on his parents' insisting that he be taken along when his older siblings go out to visit their friends, then the parents might look forward to difficulties in training the younger child's social behavior. Eventually even the youngest child will have to go out and make his own way.

You may feel that one of your children needs extra help with some problem, and there certainly should not be a rule against putting in effort where it is needed. But whose effort are we talking about? When little sister won't go out and play with others and big sister is told to take her out, who is doing the child-rearing job? There is nothing wrong with asking the big sister to help, but that help will have to receive some appreciation, which should be planned for. As we have emphasized, the children should learn to pitch in and take as much responsibility as they can—but not for nothing and not if it means that the parents lose sight of their responsibility for the child rearing.

## Making Cooperation Pay

When rules about consequences are first constructed, the question that arises is "What members of the family will be allowed to control the consequences?" With a token-economy program based on money there may be no confusion, because the parents presumably control all the money that will be given out. But when dealing with other behaviors—attention-getting behaviors, for example—other members of the family also have the power to provide consequences. The other members of the family can be informed of how the parents are trying to control the behavior, and they can also be praised, encouraged, and rewarded when they act in a helpful way.

In the process they may learn some important rules about social behaviors. In this way, other members of the family can gain from the use of a strategy. This opportunity to observe the strategy from both sides can educate a person about how the rules affect him and how he uses his own rules to affect others. Although younger members of the family may use this information to rub in the lack of or removal of positive consequences, that complication is more than offset by what they learn about their own behavior and its consequences.

Thus, when the little brother finds out that his older brother must finish his homework in order to watch TV, he may react by saying, "Ha, ha. You won't get to watch TV until you finish." But your interest should remain on the homework behavior. Make that behavior as likely as you can; the younger brother should be sent off to watch TV or whatever by himself, so that the older brother is more likely to finish and get his own payoff. Don't let your youngest child distract you from the behavior you said was important by attending to his bad behavior. If you turn too much attention to his bad behavior, then you may begin strengthening that. Possibly he needs some strategy too, but that must come from a thoughtful session, not from a reflex action to the fact that he is disrupting your rule now.

## Time Apart

Almost every child seeks some place in his home where he can be alone and where the observers or controllers of his social behaviors will not interfere. Either he has a room or place apart in the house or he uses the top of his bed as an almost sacred place in which he can be by himself. This seeking out of a free place is almost never abnormal behavior, yet sometimes parents complain about it. The child's behavior is best considered an expression of some special kind of love that he has for his home and the kind of security he finds there. If the parents think that this free place is used too much, they should consult the discussion of withdrawing in Chapter 5. But before any action is taken, the question of how trivial a problem this is should be given special attention.

### Time Together

Sometimes the modern family is so harassed by individual activities that they seem like an artificially and loosely united collection of people with no real understanding of each other. If there are such strains at the seams of family unity, the following questions may suggest some solutions. "What is your availability to the family?" "Is your availability only on your schedule or do you attempt to make some adjustments so that you are free when your children want to be with you?" "When you get together with the children, who decides the activity and subjects of conversation that will be brought up? Are these your selections or theirs?" If they are always yours, then that may partly explain why your children do not seem available very often. "Do you assume and act as if they should be the ones to be grateful for the time spent?"

All these factors and many others could influence the amount of time that the members of the family can enjoy each other's company. Also, keep in mind that it is no sin to arrange some special activity with one individual child in the family. As a matter of fact, there is much to be gained from one parent spending some period of time each week with just one child. One-to-one situations provide a time for clearer, less disrupted communication without the competition of other family members and without the need for the parents to adjust their conversation so that it is acceptable to everyone. If you are to keep up with what is going on with each child, then you will need to see each child by himself.

The old concept of family time together may not always be acceptable. To bunch everyone together for all the recreation hours of the family may actually keep communication and understanding at a minimum.

Parents can take advantage of errands to the store, individual chores, sewing time, driving to school, and so on, as times to give singular attention to one child. As a matter of fact, most parents report that their children's reactions to them are quite different and quite informative when they are not in the presence of siblings. Take advantage of moments that are free of competition. It is tempting to use these times for little talks, which are meant to straighten out the child, but you can avoid that habit. You and he can come to like these isolated moments and they can provide the setting in which the friendship between you will grow.

At first it may seem difficult to characterize "friendship" in a discussion of behaviors, but there are some immediately obvious conditions that come to mind. Surely, the establishment of friendship requires the availability of the people involved. Many persons describe friendship as "being able to count on someone," which is, to a great extent, simply being available to an individual. So when a parent begins to worry about his relationship with a child, he should consider how much time he finds to be counted on—not just for consequences, but for companionship. For that matter, when a parent begins to worry about his child's ability to establish other friendships, he might consider the availability factor and how much he influences the ability of his child to be counted on by others.

In discussing friendship, the word "understanding" usually comes up, and this concept is central to the approach taken in this book. An understanding of the rules and consequences that will occur for specific behaviors is the basis of the stability between a parent and a child. Furthermore, "understanding" might be given a broader meaning in the sense that it comes from the way in which rules are established and applied. Understanding will have to be expressed even outside the situations that directly involve the child. It will have to be expressed even in a strategy session.

In addition to "availability" and this special kind of "understanding," the word that becomes more and more important is "freedom": the freedom to be appreciated and rewarded for what you do and the freedom of those who are rapidly becoming adults to receive the responsibilities of adulthood.

From this point of view, the role of the family is to provide a gradual increase in adult responsibilities. During this development, the family protection from the outside world can have the advantage of a simpler set of rules, a fairer set of consequences, and a more reliable environment so that a child can mature with a love of life.

## OBJECTIVES *chapter eleven*

1. What is a token economy?

2. What is a contingent promotion? Why are contingent promotions important?

3. What is the "divide and conquer" approach as used by children?

4. Why are children likely to be more cautious around the father than the mother?

5. What is the possible role of relatives and siblings in a token economy?

6. Why may the old concept of family time together not be acceptable?

7. What is the role of the family as described here?

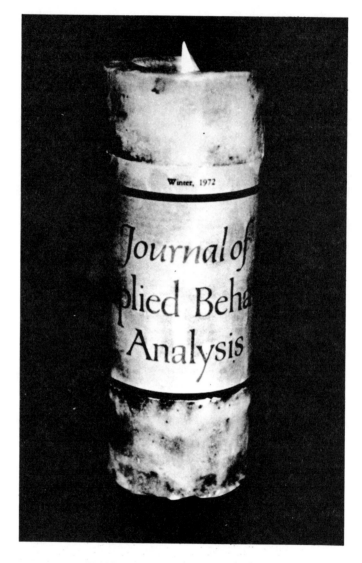

Winter, 1972

Journal of
plied Beha
Analysis

*IT IS BETTER TO LIGHT
JUST ONE LITTLE CANDLE
THAN TO CURSE THE DARKNESS*

# *Appendix*

## EXERCISE 1

### *What's Happening?*

Make two lists of your child's behaviors. The first list should be made up of the activities you don't like. Be sure each item is a real **action** of your child — not an attitude or feeling. Try to be specific. Instead of writing, "He doesn't respect me", write, "He says the following bad things to me . . ." or, "He doesn't answer me when I talk to him". Try to avoid negatives. Instead of writing, "He doesn't have the proper motivation", write, "He watches T.V. when he should be studying".

What thing does he or she do that you would like to have discontinued? Write them down as you think of them. Next, write them down a second time in their order of importance. Then, on this second list, the first behavior will be the most annoying, the one you most want to get rid of. The last behavior will be the least annoying.

Keep this list handy. We'll be coming back to it. For now, keep in mind that you rated some bad behaviors very low. Give them what they deserve — nothing: no punishment, no nagging. You have decided they are the most trivial. Don't bother yourself and your family airways with them.

List number two will be behaviors you like and hope to increase. Again, be specific and just "brain storm" the first copy. Then go back and put them in order. Save this list too.

## EXERCISE 2

### *The Logic of Consequence*

Make a list of the activities your child likes to do. This list could include behaviors from your lists in Exercise One. When you have this first list, add to it the other things that your child finds rewarding. Start with material things: Candy? Money? Books? Clothes?

Now add other rewarding events your child likes: social things, such as hugging, praise, and kisses. Copy the list over, trying to put the item your child most enjoys at the top, then the next best, etc. Keep this list handy along with the one from the first exercise. Later these things will be useful in changing behavior. And, more important, these items will help explain why the behaviors that are happening are so frequent.

## EXERCISE 3

### In Search of Meaning

Look back at the lists you made in the first exercise. Select some behavior from them that occurs frequently. Now make a small chart such as the one below and keep a record of this behavior for three days.

---

### SAMPLE CHART 1
### Behavior: Hitting Sister

| Day | Tally | Total | Comments |
|---|---|---|---|
| Monday | 𝑇𝐻𝐿 / | 6 | Regular day |
| Tuesday | 𝑇𝐻𝐿 𝑇𝐻𝐿 | 10 | Took children shopping |
| Wednesday | // | 2 | Sister was at Girl Scouts |

---

Now, look back at your lists for Exercise Two to remind yourself of the kinds of consequences to look for. Continue counting the behavior as in Chart 1, with the additional column for consequences as in Chart 2. In this chart use one whole line for each occurrence of the behavior.

---

### SAMPLE CHART 2
### Behavior: Hitting Sister

| Day | Antecedent | Consequence | Comment |
|---|---|---|---|
| Thursday | Children watching T.V. | Scolded him when he hit | Sister smiled |
| Thursday | Right after scolding | Scolded him again and told sister to stop smiling | |
| Friday | Dinner | Sent him to his room | Father went up to see how he was |

---

The purpose here is to find out what usually happens next. What is the ordinary consequence.

Do not plan a new consequence yet — just collect the information. Even when the usual consequence is obvious, it is useful to count the occurrences to see how often the "usual" consequence actually happens.

After several days of observation, begin counting what happens **before** (antecedents) as well as after (consequences). What usually leads to the behavior? That is, what antecedent did you see most often? What consequence occurred most often? How many consequences are there? Who's giving them?

## EXERCISE 4

### A Price Tag on Behavior

Select a behavior of your child's from your list. State a specific rule about the behavior — the rule should define the behavior, and state its consequence.

**Examples**
1.    If you wash the dishes by 7 p.m. you can watch T.V.
2.    If you come to dinner when called, you may eat in the dining room with the family.
3.    If you want dessert, you must taste all foods served.

Make a list of several tasks you want your child to learn (or do). Plan the conditions of practice for each task so that his chances of performing successfully are high.

**Examples**

| Task | Practice Conditions | Consequence |
|------|---------------------|-------------|
| Setting the table | Utensils, plates, etc. all within reach of child | Allowance money, praise |
| Homework | Quiet, uncluttered area for child to work in | |

## EXERCISE 5

### Punishment

Prepare a list similar to the list for Exercise Two. In this case, order the punishments you use. Remember to include specifics on reprimands, scoldings, yelling, looking mad, taking away privileges, etc.

Now for three days make a daily record of the use of these punishments as in the following example:

---

### SAMPLE CHART

| Day | Time | Behavior | Punishment |
|---|---|---|---|
| Saturday | 9:00 a.m. | Fighting | Reprimand, sent to room |
| Saturday | 11:30 a.m. | Cursing | Made him come in |
| Saturday | 12:15 p.m. | Throwing food | Made him leave table |
| Saturday | 1:30 p.m. | Refusing nap | Spanking |

---

As you fill in the chart think of what the good behavior should have been. Was any part of the good behavior exhibited before the failure? If so, what good reward and encouragement could have been used? List these encouragements as in the sample below:

---

### SAMPLE
### Possible Praise I Could Use

1. "That's good of you to share with Tommy."
2. "You sure have used a fork well since you were five."
3. "Dad said you were good about your nap Friday."

---

## EXERCISE 6

### Strategies for Success

Look back on your list from Exercise One and devise a chart to be used in helping your child keep his room clean as in the sample below:

| SAMPLE | | | | | |
|---|---|---|---|---|---|
| Chore | Date | | | | |
| | Mon. | Tues. | Weds. | Thurs. | Fri. |
| Made bed | Yes | Yes | No | Yes | Yes |
| All clothes off floor | Yes | No | | | |
| Furniture dusted | | | | | |
| Closet straight-ened | | | | | |

Look back on your list from Exercise One and pick a specific task that you would like your child to learn. Break the task down into small, uncomplicated steps. As the child completes each step successfully, move on to the next.

**Example: Baking a cake; start with a simple recipe.**

1. Assembling ingredients.
2. Assembling utensils.
3. Measuring.
4. Mixing.
5. Operating oven.
6. Timing the baking.
7. Testing the baking.
8. Removing the cake with pot holders.
9. Placing the hot cake in a safe place.

## EXERCISE 7

### Social Problems

List the opportunities your child has to be with others and count them for three days as in the chart below:

| SAMPLE | |
|---|---|
| **Day** | **Opportunity** |
| Monday | School |
| Monday | Has friends over |
| Tuesday | School |
| Tuesday | Calls friend |
| Wednesday | School |
| Wednesday | Cousin comes over |
| Wednesday | Children do homework together |

Looking back on your record, do you see any opportunity for you to make socializing easier or more frequent for your child?

## EXERCISE 8

### Giving Attention

Make out a list of the ways you give attention to your child along with the usual behaviors that precede it. Look back on your previous lists for reminders. Some examples are given below:

---

### SAMPLE

| Behavior | Attention Given |
| --- | --- |
| Spills food | Yelling, cleaning up |
| Finishes homework | Praise, read over her work |
| Picks nose | Reprimand |
| Dresses sloppily | Glare at her, compare her to others |
| Curses | Talk to her father about her with her listening |
| Helps with dishes | Talk to her |
| Gets up on time | Ask her to work |

---

Now set up a similar chart and record the frequency of these occasions of attention for three days. How often is attention given for good behavior? How often is attention given for bad behavior? Who gave most of the attention for each of these?

## EXERCISE 9

### Areas of Responsibilities

Make up a large chart for a convenient place in the kitchen. Possibly on the back of a door or on a bulletin board. List realistic chores that your children can do each day and state a portion of their allowance for each. Possibly you will want to assign particular jobs to particular children as in the sample below:

| SAMPLE Kitchen Chart for Susan | | | | | | | |
|---|---|---|---|---|---|---|---|
| | Mon | Tue | Wed | Thur | Fri | Sat | Sun |
| Make bed | | | | | | | |
| Prepare lunch | 25¢ | | | | | | |
| Clean room | | | | | | | |
| Clear dinner table | | 15¢ | | | | | |
| Wash dinner dishes | | | | | | | |
| Dry dinner dishes | | | | | | | |
| Mow lawn | | | | | | $1 | |
| Fold clothes from dryer | 50¢ | | | | | | 50¢ |
| Iron — 30 minutes | | | | | | | |
| Wash car | | | | | | | $1 |

Now plan the areas where the money can be spent. Remember a six-year-old doesn't care about money if it's going to be a week before anyone takes him to a store he likes.

## *EXERCISE 10*

### *Independence*

Make up a list of responsibilities all adults should have **and** the ages when you believe these responsibilities should be assumed. Remember to get down to some specifics as in the sample below. Make your list long and complete.

---

### SAMPLE
### Independence List

| Responsibility | Age |
|---|---|
| Bedtime | 11? |
| Homework with no parent concern | 10? |
| Toilet training | 3? |
| Bath frequency | 8? |
| Selecting clothes to wear | 7? |
| Buying clothes with no parental control | 12? |
| Time to come home in evening | 16? |
| Bed making | 6? |
| Toys picked up | 4? |
| Deciding to take (or continue) music lessons | 13? |

CONTINUE!

---

As you look back on your list remember that if you have not met your own deadline a slow building of responsibility with rewards is necessary regardless of age. You can't just demand learning! Also remember that the test of responsibility is whether or not the decisions work out **for your child.** Your way isn't the only successful way to live. Move over a little, show tolerance in judging "success".

## EXERCISE 11

### Family

After dinner one evening have each member of the family list the behaviors they most like about each other person. Then ask each person to list how they support those behaviors. Some members of the family may wish to go further and count how often they actually use these rewards that express their encouragement. Possibly the family could list ways to encourage people to encourage other's behavior.

# Footnotes

[1] Hall, R.V., Axelrod, S., Tyler, L., Grief, E., Jones, C., and Robertson, R. "Modification of behavior problems in the home with a parent as observer and experimenter." **Journal of Applied Behavior Analysis.** 1972, 5, 53-64.

[2] Zeilberger, J., Sampen, S.E., and Sloane, H. "Modification of a child's problem behaviors in the home with the mother as therapist." **Journal of Applied Behavior Analysis.** 1968, 1, 47-53.

[3] Lattal, K.A. "Contingency management of tooth-brushing behavior in a summer camp for children." **Journal of Applied Behavior Analysis.** 1973, 6, 391-396.

[4] Kohlenberg, R., and Phillips, T. "Reinforcement and rate of litter depositing." **Journal of Applied Behavior Analysis.** 1969, 2, 195-198.

[5] O'Connor, R.D. "Modification of social withdrawal through symbolic modeling." **Journal of Applied Behavior Analysis.** 1969, 2, 15-22.

[6] Wahler, R.G. "Oppositional children: A quest for parental reinforcement control." **Journal of Applied Behavior Analysis.** 1969, 2, 159-170.

[7] Broden, M., Bruce, C., Mitchell, M.A., Carter, V., and Hall, R.V. "Effects of teacher attention on attending behavior of two boys at adjacent desks." **Journal of Applied Behavior Analysis.** 1970, 3, 199-203.

[8] Christophersen, E.R., Arnold, C.M., Hills, D.W., and Quilitch, H.R. "Token reinforcement procedures for application by parents of children with behavior problems." **Journal of Applied Behavior Analysis.** 1972, 5, 485-497.

[9] Mann, R.A. "The behavior-therapeutic use of contingency contracting to control an adult behavior problem: Weight control." **Journal of Applied Behavior Analysis.** 1972, 5, 99-109.

[10] O'Brien, F. and Azrin, N.H. "Behavioral engineering: Control of posture by informational feedback." **Journal of Applied Behavior Analysis.** 1970, 3, 235-240.

[11] Powell, J.R., and Azrin, N.H. "The effects of shock as a punisher for cigarette smoking." **Journal of Applied Behavior Analysis.** 1968, 1, 68-71.

[12] Everett, P.B., Hayward, S.C., and Meyers, A.W. "The effects of a token reinforcement procedure on bus ridership." **Journal of Applied Behavior Analysis.** 1974, 7, 1-9.

[13] Knight, M.F., and McKenzie, H.S. "Elimination of bedtime thumbsucking in home settings through contingent reading." **Journal of Applied Behavior Analysis.** 1974, 7, 33-38.

[14] Ayllon, T., and Robert, M.D. "Eliminating discipline problems by strengthening academic performance." **Journal of Applied Behavior Analysis.** 1974, 7, 71-76.

[15] Johnson, S.M., and Lebitz, G.K. "Parental manipulation of child behavior in home observations." **Journal of Applied Behavior Analysis.** 1974, 7, 23-31.

[16] Bailey, J.S., Wolf, M.M., and Phillips, E.L. "Home-based reinforcement and the modification of pre-delinquents' classroom behavior." **Journal of Applied Behavior Analysis.** 1970, 3, 223-233.

[17] Lovaas, O.I., and Simmons, J.Q., MD "Manipulation of self-destruction in three retarded children." **Journal of Applied Behavior Analysis.** 1969, 2, 143-157.

[18] Birnbrauer, J.S. "Generalization of punishment effect — A case study." **Journal of Applied Behavior Analysis.** 1968, 1, 201-211.

[19] Morganstern, K.P. "Cigarette smoke as a noxious stimulus in self-managed aversion therapy for compulsive eating: Technique and case illustration." **Behavior Therapy.** 1974, 5, 255-260.

[20] Azrin, N.H., Rubin, H., O'Brien, F., Ayllon, T., and Roll, D. "Behavioral engineering: Postural control by a portable operant apparatus." **Journal of Applied Behavior Analysis.** 1968, 1, 99-108.

[21] Madsen, C.H., Becker, W.C., Thomas, D.R. "Rules, praise and ignoring: Elements of elementary classroom control." **Journal of Applied Behavior Analysis.** 1968, 1, 139-150.

[22] McReynolds, L.V. "Application of time out from positive reinforcement for increasing the efficiency of speech training." **Journal of Applied Behavior Analysis.** 1969, 2, 199-205.

[23] Ramp, E., Ulrich, R.E., and Dulaney, S. "Delayed time out as a procedure for reducing disruptive classroom behavior: A case study." **Journal of Applied Behavior Analysis.** 1971, 4, 235-239.

[24] Yen, S., McIntire, R.W., and Berkowitz, S. "Extinction of inappropriate sleeping behavior: Multiple assessment." **Psychological Reports.** 1972, 30, 375-378.

[25] Yen, S., and McIntire, R.W. "Operant therapy for constant headache complaints: A simple response-cost approach." **Psychological Reports.** 1971, 28, 267-270.

[26] Foxx, R.M., and Azrin, N.H. "The elimination of autistic self-stimulatory behavior by overcorrection." **Journal of Applied Behavior Analysis.** 1973, 6, 1-14.

[27] Herbert, E. W., and Baer, D.M. "Training parents as behavior modifiers: Self-recording of contingent attention." **Journal of Applied Behavior Analysis.** 1972, 5, 139-149.

[28] Corey, J.R., and Shamow, J. "The effects of fading on the acquisition and retention of oral reading." **Journal of Applied Behavior Analysis.** 1972, 5, 311-315.

[29] Azrin, N.H., and Powell, J. "Behavioral engineering: The reduction of smoking behavior by a conditioning apparatus and procedure." **Journal of Applied Behavior Analysis.** 1968, 1, 193-200.

[30] Surratt, P.R., Ulrich, R.E., and Hawkins, R.P. "An elementary student as a behavioral engineer." **Journal of Applied Behavior Analysis.** 1969, 2, 85-92.

[31] Sherman, T.M., and Cormier, W.H. "An investigation of the influence of student behavior on teacher behavior." **Journal of Applied Behavior Analysis.** 1974, 7, 11-21.

[32] Barrish, H.H., Saunder, M., and Wolf, M.M. "Good behavior game: Effects of individual contingencies for group consequences on disruptive behavior in the classroom." **Journal of Applied Behavior Analysis.** 1969, 2, 119-124.

[33] Cantrell, R.P., Cantrell, M.L., Huddleston, C.M., and Wooldridge, R.L. "Contingency contracting with school problems." **Journal of Applied Behavior Analysis.** 1969, 2, 215-220.

[34] Skiba, E.A., Pettigrew, E. and Alden, S.E. "A behavioral approach to the control of thumbsucking in the classroom." **Journal of Applied Behavior Analysis.** 1971, 4, 121-125.

[35] Lakey, B.B., McNees, M.P., and McNees, M.C. "Control of an obscene 'verbal tic' through time out in an elementary school classroom." **Journal of Applied Behavior Analysis.** 1973, 6, 101-104.

[36] Leitenberg, H., Agras, W., Thompson, L., and Wright, D. "Feedback in behavior modification: An experimental analysis in two phobic cases." **Journal of Applied Behavior Analysis.** 1968, 1, 131-137.

[37] Reisinger, J.J. "The treatment of 'anxiety-depression' via positive reinforcement and response cost." **Journal of Applied Behavior Analysis.** 1972, 5, 125-130.

[38] Nordquist, V.M. "The modification of a child's enuresis: Some response-response relationships." **Journal of Applied Behavior Analysis.** 1971, 4, 241-247.

[39] Hall, R. V., Custler, C., Craston, J.S., and Toucker, B. "Teachers and parents as researchers using multiple baseline designs." **Journal of Applied Behavior Analysis.** 1970, 3, 247-255.

[40] Bailey, J.S., Timbers, G.D., Phillips, E.L., and Wolf, M.M. "Modification of articulation errors of pre-delinquents by their peers." **Journal of Applied Behavior Analysis.** 1971, 4, 265-281.

[41] Wilson, C.W., and Hopkins, B.L. "The effects of contingent music on the intensity of noise in junior high home economics classes." **Journal of Applied Behavior Analysis.** 1973, 6, 269-275.

[42] Long, J.D., and Williams, R.L. "The comparative effectiveness of group and individually contingent free time with inner-city junior high school students." **Journal of Applied Behavior Analysis.** 1973, 6, 465-474.

[43] MacDonald, W.S., Gallimore, R., and MacDonald, G. "Contingency counseling by school personnel: An economical model of intervention." **Journal of Applied Behavior Analysis.** 1970, 3, 175-182.

[44] Jones, R.J., and Azrin, N.H. "An experimental application of a social reinforcement approach to the problem of job-finding." **Journal of Applied Behavior Analysis.** 1973, 6, 345-353.

[45] Miller, L.K., and Miller, O.L. "Reinforcing self-help group activities of welfare recipients." **Journal of Applied Behavior Analysis.** 1970, 3, 57-64.

[46] McLaughlin, T.F., and Malaby, J. "Intrinsic reinforcers in a classroom token economy." **Journal of Applied Behavior Analysis.** 1972, 5, 263-270.

# Suggestions for further reading

Atkinson, Butler M. *What Dr. Spock Didn't Tell Us: Or, A Survival Kit for Parents.* New York: Simon and Schuster, 1959.

Ayllon, Teodoro, and Nathan H. Azrin. *The Token Economy.* New York: Appleton-Century-Crofts, 1969.

Bugelski, Richard B. *The Psychology of Learning as Applied to Teaching.* Indianapolis: Bobbs-Merrill, 1964.

Chapman, A. H. *A Guide for Perplexed Parents.* Philadelphia: Lippincott, 1966.

Crow, Lester D., and Alice Crow. *Being a Good Parent.* Boston: Christopher Publishing House, 1966.

Edge, Patricia. *Child Care and Management from Pre-natal Days to Adolescence.* New York: Transatlantic, 1966.

Gersh, Marvin. *How to Raise Children at Home in Your Spare Time.* New York: Stein and Day, 1966.

Ginott, Haim G. *Between Parent and Child.* New York: Macmillan, 1965.

Hauch, Paul A. *The Rational Management of Children.* New York: Libra Publishers, 1967.

Ilg, Frances L., and Louise B. Ames. *The Gesell Institute's Child Behavior.* New York: Dell, 1960.

LeShan, Eda J. *How to Survive Parenthood.* New York: Random House, 1965.

Mayer, Greta, and Mary Hoover. *Learning to Love and Let Go.* New York: Child Study Association of America, 1965.

Patterson, Gerald R., and M. Elizabeth Guillion. *Living with Children.* Champaign, Ill.: Research Press, 1969.

Piers, Maria W. *Growing Up with Children.* Chicago: Quadrangle Books, 1966.

Reese, Ellen P. *The Analysis of Human Operant Behavior.* Dubuque: W. C. Brown, 1966.

Skinner, B. F. *Science and Human Behavior.* New York: Macmillan, 1953.
———. *The Technology of Teaching.* New York: Appleton-Century-Crofts, 1968.

Smart, Mollie S., and Russell C. Smart. *Living and Learning with Children.* Boston: Houghton Mifflin, 1961.

Smith, Elinor G. *The Complete Book of Absolutely Perfect Baby and Child Care.* New York: Harcourt, Brace & World, 1957.

Smith, Judith M., and Donald E. P. Smith. *Child Management: A Program for Parents.* Ann Arbor: Ann Arbor Publishers, 1966.

Whaley, Donald L., and Richard W. Malott. *Elementary Principles of Behavior*. Englewood Cliffs: Prentice-Hall, 1970.

Woody, Robert H. *Behavioral Problem Children in the Schools*. New York: Appleton-Century-Crofts, 1969.

# Index